READINGS IN GENERAL MUSIC

Selected reprints from *Soundings*,
a publication of the
Society for General Music, 1982 to 1987

Music Educators National Conference

Table of Contents

Foreword

The Society for General Music (SGM) was established in 1982 to meet the concerns of those members of the Music Educators National Conference (MENC) whose primary interest is the general music education of all our nation's youth. It was also organized to meet the need for a stronger "general music" voice within MENC. The ultimate goal of the society is to have every student in America experience music in ways that will broaden and deepen their lives. Five objectives for achieving this goal are:

1. To provide for the development of a comprehensive general music program for all ages
2. To bring the purpose of general music education into clear focus for the educational community and general public
3. To provide leadership that speaks directly to the needs of the general music educator
4. To identify the commonalities that bind all special interest groups functioning within general music education and to utilize the unique contributions of each
5. To offer a strong national forum for ideas and approaches to general music at all levels of learning

Soundings evolved as one of the strategies for addressing the SGM goal and objectives. It appeared as a small quarterly publication dealing with topics of specific interest to general music teachers. Philosophical and pragmatic issues were treated in articles along with strategies for general music. Mary Val Marsh was the original editor.

At its meeting in January 1987, the SGM Executive Board requested that MENC provide general music teachers with an expanded and more substantive publication, *General Music Today*. At the same time, concern emerged for preserving many of the articles and teaching strategies that appeared in *Soundings,* which was published by MENC in the form of a pamphlet. This format did not lend itself to easy storage and retrieval; the issues could easily be lost even in personal libraries. Thus, retaining selected articles in a more permanent publication seemed important.

Readings in General Music is organized by topics. Individual articles have been reformatted for consistency, but editorial content has not been changed. This book presents a variety of articles and teaching strategies for music educators who teach general music classes in elementary, middle or junior high, and senior high schools.

Lenore Pogonowski, Compiler

SECTION ONE

GENERAL MUSIC ISSUES

General Music— What Is It?

Eloise Haldeman

How many of us have heard people say "I don't know much about music, but I know what I like and don't like!"? We cringe when we hear such a statement, not only because of the ignorance revealed, but because it points to a commonly held attitude that music is merely to be enjoyed, not understood. Ignorance may be bliss and, of course, people have a right to their own opinions, but the idea of making choices without knowledge runs counter to the entire purpose of education, including music education.

General music is one aspect of music education. But what is "general music"? At the 1981 MENC Conference in Minneapolis, then-President Mary E. Hoffman said that general music is the heart, the vital center, of the music program. Some say that it is the "meat and potatoes" of the music program. Others describe general music as the trunk of the tree, that is, the main body of musical study, out of which grow the limbs of performance opportunities for those with special interests and talents. To some, general music is the music instruction given in elementary K-6 classrooms by classroom teachers, music specialists, or a combination of the two. To others, it is a name given to classes offered in middle, junior high, and senior high schools for those students who do not participate in performing ensembles. To still others, general music is a concept that includes these descriptions and is expanded to embrace preschool, K-12, higher education, and continued lifelong musical learning. Is it possible that general music is all of these, and more?

Performing ensembles are usually thought of as a separate facet of music education because they are based on special interests, talents, and skills, or because they teach primarily those skills and concepts necessary to the performance of music that is within the capabilities of the performers. Exceptions do exist, however; some teachers also work to transfer performance skills, understandings and germinal aesthetic criteria to (a) analyses of repertoire and media different from those encountered through performance, and to (b) creative endeavors involving improvisation and composition. Such a comprehensive approach frequently takes more time than is available, so performers are left with gaps in their musical experiences, gaps that need to be filled.

How did the idea of general music evolve? We all know that in 1838 Lowell Mason persuaded the Boston School Board to incorporate music into the public school curriculum. At that time, school music consisted of learning to sing and to read notation. It was more than sixty years later, at the turn of the century, that school orchestras came into existence, and they were comprised of students who already knew how to play their instruments. Thanks to the influence of schools in England, in which violin classes were being taught, violin and other instrumental classes for beginners were added to American schools about 1910; at this time the development of school bands also got under way. Piano classes were initiated a few years later. The player piano and especially the invention of the phonograph led, in the second decade of this century, to the teaching of listening lessons for the purpose of developing music appreciation.

According to Edward Birge (*History of Public School Music in the United States*, MENC, first edition, 1928), important issues at that time were (1) the relationship of appreciation studies to already established school music education; (2) whether music appreciation was a "body of knowledge" or "an attitude of mind"; (3) at what grade levels listening lessons were most appropriate; and (4) whether "true appreciation" came solely from listening lessons or "from actual participation in the music, through singing or playing from the printed notation."

Birge wrote further that almost everyone believed that listening lessons were "a motivating force in the study of music, whatever form the study took," and "agreed that children should have as much opportunity as possible to hear good music." At the same time, student field trips to symphony concerts and the music (listening) memory test became popular. To round out this short sketch of the history of public school music it should be noted that at a national meeting of school superintendents held in March of 1927, it was resolved that "we are rightly coming to regard music, art, and other similar subjects as fundamental in the education of American children...[and]...that they be given everywhere equal consideration and support with other basic subjects."

Birge's book may have been written in the 1920s, but it is certainly not out of date, and the issues of those times seem to have startling relevancy to the 1980s. Since 1928 there has been a mind-boggling array of new developments, including all kinds of learning theories, programs for early childhood, identification of and programs for the gifted and talented, innovative and resurrected (exhumed?) music education methodologies, growth of the mass media and audiovisual industries, advanced electronic technologies, new and improved musical instruments, a wide variety of new music, and so on. It is to be hoped that knowledge of the past will prevent us from trying to reinvent the wheel and enable us to get on with our task of defining general music and codifying its goals and standards in today's world.

But the question remains: What is general music? Is it possible to create a Gestalt, a larger framework that encompasses comprehensive, in-depth and quality musical learning; that allows those in performing ensembles to study and to become acquainted with music that is beyond their performance ability; that can be adapted within a pluralistic society to fit the needs of local areas and populations; that leads all learners, within their abilities, to develop understandings, appreciations, and aesthetic sensibilities—not only in music, but also in other arts and in the humanities—that will continue to grow during their lifetimes?

Yes, it is possible. If we musicians/teachers will commit ourselves to larger goals, to a spirit of cooperation, and to respect for one another's roles in the whole of music education, then we will find ways to convert this amorphous idea called "general music" into an inspiring totality that will become greater than the sum of its parts.

Eloise Haldeman is supervisor of elementary (K-8) music in the Beverly Hills Unified school District, Beverly Hills, California.

Problems Facing General Music Today

Sally Monsour

Problems are not new to music education in general, nor to general music in particular. Traditional problems, however, are being seen in a new perspective in light of current societal conditions. For instance, decreasing enrollments and budget cuts are forcing many teachers and administrators to justify the general music program in concrete ways. When such a situation arises, it seems prudent to look to causal factors and relationships for constructive help.

To this end the Georgia chapter of the Society for General Music attempted to define and rank problems that general music teachers presently perceive as important. At the most recent GMEA conference, in an elementary session, problems were posed and subsequently ranked by teachers from a variety of locations in the state. While the number reporting was not large, the response was representative of all levels and types of programs. Considerable time at the meeting was given for discussion; thus, it was felt that the results were based on thoughtful inquiry.

Teachers were asked to rank the following nine problems as *extremely important, important or less important*. In addition, they were requested to place a plus sign next to the problem considered most important.

1. Setting realistic goals—feeling comfortable with student achievement.
2. Relationship of the music program to other school areas.
3. Scheduling.
4. Building a better understanding among music teachers at all levels.

5

5. Motivating students in music.

6. Eliciting creative responses within a comprehensive approach, given time limitations.

7. Classroom management and discipline.

8. Maintaining teacher interest and enthusiasm (i.e., burnout).

9. Individualizing instruction with minimal resources.

Problem Number One

The problem that was ranked as most critical was: "Setting realistic goals, i.e., feeling comfortable with student achievement." While this came as no surprise, one is tempted to ask why, with all our recent stress on behaviors and objectives, goal-setting still eludes us.

One reason is that we have minimal instructional time and have set for ourselves too many goals. What is more, these goals are not always based on an accurate appraisal of student progress. Also, the array of methodologies we are "supposed" to be using only serves to confuse means and ends—with too many means resulting in too few satisfying ends. But, whatever the cause, the problem of goal attainment is one of the most serious; doubly so because it is directly linked to another problem that we are hearing with increasing frequency—that public and administrative perceptions of general music are unclear and full of misconceptions. This, in turn, results in lack of support.

The times call for clarifying what we do in the classroom, particularly as related to those aspects of the program that result in benefits over a person's lifetime. Setting goals within the curriculum to include what we feel we can do *well* is the order of the day. Then, we will be in a position to send up flares in the community as a signal of student progress in music making and learning. That was precisely what Lowell Mason did and it worked.

Motivation

Another problem that was ranked very high in our Georgia survey was motivation. "Why, oh why," one asks, "should motivation be a problem in teaching such a glorious and generally popular subject as music?" We are all aware that children normally like music. It is naturally motivating. So musical involvement linked to the student's developmental interests should "hit the nail on the head."

The key to the problem of motivation is the day-to-day assurance that the content of the musical selections is interesting and that the student's experience is rewarding. It has been observed over and over that when obstacles between the student and the music itself are taken away, students tend to be motivated. It is **we** who are charged with clearing such paths to learning.

Surely there are situations in which one or more of the above problems do not exist, where there is a reasonable amount of time for instruction, where goals are set in realistic terms, and where students are motivated in the general music class. But, where serious problems do exist, they can loom very large for the individual music teacher. In situations where problems are linked to factors outside the teacher's control, solutions seem remote.

With this in mind, creativity in problem solving is the order of the day. Initiative—not timidity—is called for. Groups such as the Society for General Music can help provide the communicative link. Bring your ideas, whoever and wherever you are, and join us in capturing a significant place for music in the general education of our students.

Sally Monsour is Professor of Music, Georgia State University, Atlanta.

Quality in Music Education

Gerard L. Knieter

American education is a microcosm of American society. It is, therefore, subject to the same stress factors that infect our entire population. Our failure to manage the economy in general, and specific industries in particular, has led us to question the whole educational enterprise. It is important to note that concern for American education did not become a public matter until the "free speech movement" in the 1960's and until the economy in the past two decades focused attention upon cost. While it is true that the American family claims a basic commitment to education, it is common knowledge that serious budget cuts have been felt throughout the educational spectrum.

Cries for quality, or excellence, in education are endorsed by both political parties since such commitments are among the easiest to embrace during a campaign. Such political manipulations were observed when the Secretary of Education was brought to Washington to dismantle the Department of Education. Next, he strongly supported education when it became a campaign issue. Recently he resigned when it became obvious that insufficient financial support would be available to provide an appropriate basis for either present or new programs.

However, the idea that Americans are concerned with excellence is useful, as it allows us to demonstrate that the nature of our public accountability (performance) has been an historic professional commitment. From the very beginning, teachers and students have spent

7

their time together working towards perfection. Since music is an academic discipline with a performance component, we have been able to illustrate excellence as an ongoing process.

It is important for us to identify what quality in music education is, so that we can have a frame of reference for the purpose of both setting our goals and assessing our efforts. Quality, or excellence, is the highest level of expression possible from an individual or group, which is characteristic of the normative criteria of a discipline or field. Expression is understood to mean any act, event, or process in which teachers, student, administrators and supervisors may be involved. This definition presupposes that the reader is knowledgeable about the process of education. It assumes that teachers understand that it is their responsibility to design an environment which is conducive to learning; that learning involves a change in behavior; and that the interactive process between the two takes place at all ages, levels of instruction, and in the classroom, studio, and concert hall. Excellence is a pluralistic construct in music education; it applies equally to the elementary classroom specialist whose challenges are infinite and to the college professor teaching the doctoral seminar where the challenge may be highly focused in a narrow area of research. It is a point of view which requires each of us, and our students, to produce "the highest level of expression possible" and, therefore, enables our profession to embrace quality as a fundamental component of the teaching/learning process in music education.

Since the American public has been oriented to the importance of excellence in education, it now becomes possible for music educators to take a proactive position with respect to accountability. While it is customary for parents to be invited to concerts, we should now take the opportunity to invite them to our general music classes where the mystery of music is explored through composition, performance, and appreciation (evaluation). It would be useful for the community to hear the compositions composed by elementary and middle school children. Through the use of the tape recorder and computer, as well as the more traditional instruments and approaches, the instructional process in music today rivals the most sophisticated left brain activities commonly associated with science and mathematics. Yet, we tend to share only performance with the community. The time has come for us to open our general music classes to the public so that more people can become aware of the ways in which music as an academic discipline is learned.

Quality is generally viewed as a goal which tends to improve musical learning for students. But it is a much more pervasive idea. It is a commitment every music educator makes by becoming a self-instructional agent. We are the "physicians of music." As such, our mission involves the cultivation of our own musical and educational skill and knowledge so that we can enjoy the role and excitement of continuing to be active learners. This is easy to say but it involves risks. It means asking simple questions, as students so often do, such as: "What is music?" "How can you tell a good piece from a bad one?" and, "Why is it that no one has evolved a comprehensive philosophy of music education that most of us can understand, explain to colleagues, and use as a rationale at the national level?"

The risk is that asking questions and encouraging our students to ask questions often places us in what is traditionally perceived as a vulnerable position. This process reveals the underlying assumptions upon which our entire understanding of music and all that impinges upon the instructional process rests. Since both our society and the educational institutions in which we were indoctrinated encourage conformity, we have learned not to question. Hence, we do not encourage our students to question. But, a commitment to quality requires questions!

Our discipline is an art. It is an art which exists in time. Music is an evolving art reflective of the personality of the composer and performer while characteristic of the social ethos. We are blessed and cursed because, while our responsibilities to students may not be of a life-threatening nature, they do impact on the quality of life. What is being proposed is that our commitment to excellence requires a new investigation into the nature of musical meaning. To date we can review the Wagner-Hanslick debates, the tiresome referential vs. non-referential arguments, or escape into 19th Century Langerian Symbolism where circular reasoning in musical matters reaches its zenith. We have not examined the nature of musical expression as an evolving construct for the 21st Century. For too long we have allowed the philosopher and the aesthetician to tell us what music means. The reason we are unhappy with all of the explanations is that they really do not deal with music. And, our intuition as musicians tells us that they (the philosophical explanations) are wrong.

In the midst of the political and educational debates now underway, our long commitment to quality can be publicized and exploited. Hence, while the public and our colleagues from other fields talk about this "new" idea, we welcome the opportunity to share our approaches to the teaching and learning of music with those who are best informed. There are few educational innovations that have not been tried first by music educators. It is important for us to establish the fact that our profession has been oriented to excellence since ancient times and that this commitment has continued into the present.

Finally, we know that music education in American schools is an example of quality, for we have developed the most impressive approach to large group instrumental and choral teaching in the world. There are more and better bands, orchestras and choruses in our schools *per capita* than anywhere else on the planet. Innovations in the teaching of general music and in curriculum development share the same impressive background since the study of music is viewed from all styles, periods, and cultures. *Quality, or excellence, in music education depends upon the degree to which every student has the opportunity to compose, to perform, and to appreciate (evaluate) music.* Music educators are committed to quality because the demands of our art require it, and because we have chosen to share this art with others.

Gerard L. Knieter is professor of music and dean of the College of Fine and Applied Arts at The University of Akron and adjunct professor of behavioral sciences at the Northeastern Ohio Universities College of Medicine.

SECTION TWO

PROCESS MODELS

The Art of Questioning

Gail Hynes and Jack W. Kukuk

Skillful questioning by the teacher in the classroom is truly an art. A question can elicit a poorly thought-out one word answer, or it can challenge the student to participate actively in a dialogue that requires creative thinking and clarity of communication.

We as music teachers spend much time determining concepts to be explored and materials to be used in our lesson plans. Seldom, however, do we give conscious, deliberate thought to the manner in which questions will be delivered. We tend to "improvise" questions. If the students seem puzzled, we surmise that we need to restate the question until the desired response is obtained.

Many of our questions do not challenge creative response because they require only one answer. We tend to call upon the few students who are adept at answering questions, thus depriving the majority from participating in discussion.

The following material has been excerpted from the publication "IMAGINATION: The Springboard to Creativity," prepared by the John F. Kennedy Center for the Performing Arts Education Program, and has been adapted to provide some guidelines for the general music teacher.

Introduction to Creative Questioning

In most instances teachers ask convergent questions, questions which call for a correct response. These questions are necessary in that they allow a teacher to know whether a student possesses a certain body of knowledge or has acquired a specific skill. However, convergent questions will not make the student think creatively. A creative, or divergent question is an open-ended question that does not have a correct answer or response. When a teacher asks a divergent question it forces a student to use his/her own resources to create an answer.

Every classroom needs a balance between these two types of questions, but it is important to remember that a student must have the knowledge and skills necessary to the subject before proceeding to divergent questioning.

The following section addresses three types of divergent questions. They are: fluency, flexibility, and associative thinking.

Fluency Questions

GOAL: To encourage students to see things in new ways by generating a number of alternatives and by encouraging networking.

DESCRIPTION: Fluency questions generate many new ideas on a subject by postponing judgment until all possible responses are elicited. "Far out," more creative ideas should be encouraged.

PROCEDURE:
1. Select a topic or question.
2. Record all responses.
3. Postpone all evaluations or judgments until after the session, including non-verbal judgments.
4. Encourage as many responses as possible. This gives you more alternatives to consider.
5. Encourage hitchhiking or piggybacking. One person's ideas will probably spark an idea from someone else.
6. Evaluate the ideas—remember the more "far out" responses may provide the greatest potential for creative solutions.

EXAMPLES:
•How can you communicate without using words?
•How many ways can you think of to measure time in music?
•How many musical uses can you find for a wastepaper basket?
•How many ways can you think of to direct a person to Symphony Hall?

Flexibility Questions

GOAL: To encourage students to see things in new ways and challenge assumptions.

DESCRIPTION: There are four types of flexibility questions. These involve the ability to become involved with a subject, to view a problem from different viewpoints, to consciously deceive oneself, and to reorganize existing elements.

INVOLVEMENT QUESTIONS: These questions force students to turn themselves into a living, non-living, abstract or symbolic subject by "becoming" something else. Through this type of questioning, students are released from their rigid or preconceived perceptions.

EXAMPLES:
•How would you feel if you were the water in the Sorcerer's Apprentice?

•You are "Rock Music" at a classical concert. How do you feel?
•How would you feel if you were the bus on a Mick Jagger concert tour?

VIEWPOINT QUESTIONS: These questions allow students to see things in a different perspective or from a different point of view. Three perspectives are considered. These are: persons of different ages, classes, or personalities; different time, forward or backward; different space relations, geographical or physical perspectives. The greatest flexibility will be elicited by the most unusual or odd viewpoints.

EXAMPLES:
•What would Beethoven think of Stravinsky's style of composing?
•How would you describe the synthesizer to Bach?
•How would Columbus view the music of _____?

CONSCIOUS SELF-DECEIT QUESTIONS: By purposeful deceit, by believing that impossible conditions exist, problems and blocks can be removed thereby opening the way to create new solutions.

EXAMPLES:
•If you had the ability to write the world's greatest music, what style would you use?
•If you could have Mozart answer any question, what would you ask him?
•You have been given the power to reorganize the music to which the world listens. How would you use this power to create ideal conditions?
•If you could remove or change a musical event in history, what would it be?

REORGANIZATION QUESTIONS: Reorganization questions allow us to change reality to get new insights and find ways to rethink established realities. Three ways of reorganizing reality are to: add or increase, subtract or decrease, and to reorder or reverse elements.

EXAMPLES:
•What if there were no music?
•Suppose Stevie Wonder were not blind. How would this affect his music?
•If Tchaikovsky were a rock musician, what would the consequences be?

Associative Thinking Questions

GOAL: To encourage students to make connections between unrelated actions and things and to encourage them to use chance and take advantage of the unexpected.

DESCRIPTION: Associative or forced association questions develop the ability to bring together two seemingly unrelated ideas into a new or unique combination that often possesses originality.

PROCEDURE:
1. Be sure that students have knowledge of all subjects or items being discussed.
2. Use uncommon or dissimilar items when forcing associations.
3. Unique or unusual associations should be encouraged.

EXAMPLES:
•What ideas can you get from an egg to create a musical composition?
•How is balancing a checkbook like writing music?
•How is World War II like the music of _____?

The Importance of Timing

Utilizing questioning techniques that involve fluency, flexibility, and associative thinking is important to stimulating creativity in the classroom. Equally important to the process is providing "time" for the student to formulate the answers. Rowe in her research on wait-time found that teachers, on an average, allowed only about one second for the student to answer a question. If not answered, the teacher tended to repeat, ask another question, or call on another to answer. Rowe suggests that the brief wait-time factor is a major inhibitor of the student's response.

It would then seem that our challenge as music teachers is not only to plan the nature of our questions but to be prepared to listen as the students shape and share their answers.

References:

Rowe, M.B., "Wait-time and rewards as instructional variables, their influence on language, logic and fate control. Part I: Wait-time." *Journal of Research in Science Teaching.* 1974, 2 (2), 81-94.

Rowe, M.B., "Reflections on wait-time: Some methodological questions." *Journal of Research in Science Teaching.* 1974, 11 (3), 263-279.

Rowe, M.B., "Relation of wait-time and rewards to the development of language, logic and fate control: Part II: Rewards." *Journal of Research in Science Teaching.* 1974, 11 (4), 290-308.

Our thanks to:

Gail Hynes, Jefferson County (Colorado) Public Schools Arts in Education Program.

Jack W. Kukuk, Director of Education, John F. Kennedy Center for the Performing Arts, Washington, D.C.

The Anatomy of a Creative Music Strategy

Lenore Pogonowski

People are curious by nature, whether they be children or adults, or persons falling somewhere between the ambiguous lines of childhood and adulthood. This curiosity can be viewed in the behavior of the toddler who unceasingly rearranges the lower levels of the kitchen; of the retiree who pursues new life projects; and of the elementary, middle, or senior high school student who devotes an incessant amount of time trying to master the techniques of a newly acquired electronic instrument. At all ages people seem to have a basic curiosity which motivates investigations of one sort or another. We capitalize on natural curiosity in the general music class when our plan of action—the strategy —sparks the curiosity of our students and provides them with an incentive for investigating the processes by which music is made.

A creative music strategy is a plan of action designed in such a way that students' music ideas evolve as they interact with each other and the teacher. Some students will be inventive at early stages of the plan, while other students will require external musical influences to inspire their efforts. Both types of students need time to develop their musical ideas and the skills associated with performing them. At all stages of the strategy, then, musical alternatives must be available for all students to function comfortably together.

The essence of a creative music strategy is choice. Choice relates to the opportunities students have to create and exercise musical options.

When students are making choices about the use of pitch, duration, dynamics, timbre and form, they are problem solving and practicing creative musical behavior. At the same time students are developing a myriad of skills associated with that behavior.

As students approach early adolescence, they become increasingly interested in exploring musical ideas that bear some relationship to the popular medium. Inevitably, pitch will be a major factor in strategies designed to accommodate this interest. One of the problems associated with the use of pitch is that students' musical choices are often limited by their abilities to produce musically convincing performances.

One solution for the problem is to design a long range strategy that not only invites students to think creatively with musical materials, but also supports students as they develop related skills needed to satisfy their musical expectations. Creative music strategies need time to develop. If a plan is abandoned before students have reached a level whereby they are able to perform their ideas in a musically convincing manner, future efforts in creative thinking may be stifled and opportunities for refinement through practice will be lost.

The remainder of this article will present one sequence of activities that will exemplify the progressive stages of a creative music strategy. These stages range from the establishment of an aural frame of reference to exploratory and improvisatory activities and end with a reapplication of ideas.

THE STRATEGY

The main objective of the strategy presented below is to develop melodic materials that can be harmonized with an parallel two-chord progression. Chords built on G and F will serve as the harmonic focus. All melodic materials should be constructed by students through an exploratory/improvisational process, as they try various melodic ideas in relationship to the harmonic structure.

To facilitate the participation of all students, the teacher or a student will need to provide a supportive background accompaniment **at every stage of the strategy.** The accompaniment will help students accomplish the following: (1) maintain the two-chord progression so that judgments regarding the effectiveness of melodic ideas can be made by students; (2) keep a steady tempo; and, (3) provide students with a musical environment that resembles the context into which they will eventually refine and perform their ideas. The following or a similar accompaniment pattern may be employed:

G   F

Establishing an Aural Frame of Reference

Since the principal ideas of the strategy center on the use of pitch, a harmonic frame of reference for the two-chord progression needs to be established. The teacher can do this at the piano by playing each of the G chord members, one at a time, and inviting students to select and hum a chord tone most comfortable in their range. (Piano will be assumed as the accompanying instrument; however, any instrument may be substituted to produce a chordal style accompaniment.)

The above process can be repeated with the teacher asking students to identify which of the chord tones they are humming. The question will help the students to focus on the relationship of their chord tones to the overall sound. Students may then be informed that by moving a whole step down from their starting pitches, they will automatically be singing a tone contained in the F chord. By humming, or using vocal scat sounds, students can practice moving back and forth between the two chords. They also can experiment with other chord tones as starting pitches, while the teacher plays the accompaniment pattern.

Individual Exploration

With an aural frame of reference established, students now need time for exploration with instruments, to gain basic experience needed for creating melodies. Depending upon the facilities, number of students in the class, and available instrumentation, the teacher may wish to engage the entire class in simultaneous explorations. If this is not feasible, small groups of students can take turns.

The purpose of individual exploration is similar to the purpose for asking a divergent question. Both require problem solving to create a unique answer. At this stage students will be curious about their individual abilities to create melodies. A group setting is recommended because it provides a sense of privacy for experimenting. It is not expected at this point that the resulting sound will appear to be organized.

Using pitched instruments, students should be encouraged to go beyond the G and F chord tones and experiment with a wide range of diatonic pitches to produce melodic ideas. Students can begin, as they did vocally, by choosing any one of the G chord tones as a point of departure.

Nonpitched percussion instruments can be played by student volunteers who wish to improvise rhythms or to perform from suggested patterns, such as the following:

Guided Exploration

While students were encouraged to create their own melodies in the previous stage, the purpose of guided exploration is to help them see melodic alternatives. The main source for generating these alternatives is the class. On an individual basis, each student can share his/her melody with other class members until all available melodies have been performed with accompaniment.

Students' attention to differences in the melodies can be directed with questions, such as the following: "How do the melodies differ in length?" "Does the melody move in an ascending or a descending direction, or does it move in both directions?" "What do you like best about the melody?" The questions and answers can be followed with experiments that combine melodies of different lengths and similar lengths. Other experiments can combine melodies that move in similar directions and melodies that move in contrasting directions.

A second source for generating melodic alternatives is the teacher. It should be noted, however, that if a large quantity of melodies is shared by students, the teacher may not need to suggest other possibilities. The students' melodies should be highlighted and the following material can be saved for another class or time.

Experiments can be conducted to test the effectiveness of melodic beginnings that use a single tone, and later include additional tones. For each of the experiments, the entire class may play and sing in unison with the accompaniment pattern.

Choose a single tone which can be played or sung in any comfortable octave, as for example:

Try other single tones suggested by students. In the same manner proceed, then, to a two-tone pattern and additional patterns. Rhythm and dynamics can be varied, as well as pitch.

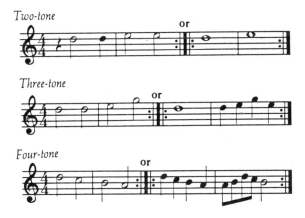

Eight repetitions of the two-measure examples, performed at a steady moderate tempo, should give students sufficient opportunity to make judgments. This will be adequate, especially if the experiments are tape recorded for playback and discussion.

The melodic beginnings suggested above may be helpful for students who have difficulty getting started. Caution needs to be exercised, however. If the patterns are used as substitutes for the students' musical ideas, the objective of the strategy will have lost much of its creative value.

In guided exploration the entire class has a single focus at all times. Students listen and analyze each other's melodies; test the effectiveness of various combined melodies; and experiment with melodic beginnings, rhythms, and dynamics. Throughout this stage attention is devoted to individuals performing a single melodic fragment to determine its effect with the two-chord progression.

Exploratory Improvisation

Exploratory improvisation resembles individual exploration from the standpoint of how the class operates. Individual exploration provided the security of a group setting. Students were free to create melodic ideas, along with other students, who also were free to utilize an approach unique to them. All students were self-centered within the group.

This stage differs from individual exploration in that a great deal of musical data has been accumulated. Students have performed their own melodies, but also, they have been exposed to many other melodic ideas from their peers, and possibly the teacher. With all the melodic data that have been generated, students need time to revise, refine, and practice their melodies so that they can feel secure about pitches, rhythms, and dynamics predictably falling into place in the course of a performance.

Exploratory improvisation is the stage at which the students have an opportunity to practice their melodic options in a group setting. Participation in the large group allows students to pursue, at their individual levels, the refinements needed to produce musically convincing performances. Whereas unison group responses were elicited for some of the experiments in the previous stage, each student will now focus on practicing the melodic material she/he is most interested in performing.

Planned Improvisation

Thoughtful questioning can assist students in planning an improvisation. Leading questions can be devised to meet specific circumstances. Some examples are the following:

"If we create for our concert a class composition based on the G-F progression, what suggestions would you have for a (1) beginning section, (2) middle section, (3) ending section?"

"Should we have any solos, duets, trios, or quartets?" "If so, where in the piece do you think they should occur?"

There is no end to the number of pertinent questions one can devise. From the questions and subsequent class discussions, there will emerge alternative plans for a class composition.

Planned improvisation is the result of the students' cumulative efforts to organize their musical ideas in a format which is musically meaningful to them. This format could evolve from a class discussion with details outlined on the chalkboard during the process. Several plans could result from the efforts of smaller groups. Other plans might surface from students wishing to conduct the class. All group and individual plans should be implemented, so that students get as much musical interaction as possible.

20

Reapplication

The final stage of the strategy is as much a beginning as it is an ending. It is an opportunity for students to refine their plans. At the same time it offers a chance to explore other combinations of musical ideas initiated by students or teacher. Students, for example, may determine that in addition to the person (student or teacher) who maintains the accompaniment pattern, a choir of guitars, Autoharps, omnichords, and mallet instruments could provide occasional color; additional interest could be obtained by including band or orchestral instruments played by class members.

The teacher could introduce melodic fragments to demonstrate contrasts such as conjunct vs. disjunct melodic motion, or syncopated vs. nonsyncopated rhythmic figures.

Examples are the following:

Time should be devoted to learning the fragments so that comparisons can be made. When some or all of the fragments are learned, students might select one with which they would like to work. Fragments could be combined, extended in length, or both.

Finally, the song *Bamboo* (page 22) could be introduced and performed with any of the musical materials that have been produced thus far in the strategy.

BAMBOO

1. You take a stick of bam-boo, You take a stick of bam-boo, You
2. You trav - el on the riv - er, You trav - el on the riv - er, You
3. My home's a-cross the riv - er, My home's a-cross the riv - er, My

take a stick of bam-boo, You throw it in the wa-ter.
trav-el on the riv - er, You trav-el on the wa - ter. Oh,___
home's a - cross the riv - er, My home's a-cross the wa - ter.

Oh,___ Han - ah.___

Chorus

Riv - er,___ she come down.___

Descant

Source could not be determined.

Summary

In the strategy just described the class functions together in some way at all stages. The way in which it functions is determined by the specific purposes of each stage. In establishing an aural frame of reference the class had a single focus on the harmonic progression. The process by which class members created melodies at the second stage was uniquely individual, both non-threatening in the large group setting. Guided exploration provided a single focus again. This time the focus was on individual performances of melodies and on musical material to stimulate further thought. Students proceeded to revise, refine, and practice their melodies in exploratory improvisation in preparation for the individual, group, and class projects at the next stage. Reapplication provided an opportunity to broaden and intensify all previous experiences with the strategy.

As suggested earlier in the article, creative music strategies need time to develop. If we invite students to participate in a creative music strategy, we must find ways within the framework of the strategy to support the development of associated skills. One of the strongest bonds between the student and the general music class is a musically convincing performance of the *student's* musical ideas.

References:

Biasini, Amercole, Pogonowski, Lenore, and Thomas, Ronald. *MMCP Interaction*, 2nd. ed. Bardonia, New York: Media Materials, Inc., 1971.

Hynes, Gail, and Kukuk, Jack, "The Art of Questioning." *Soundings*, Spring 1983, 2-2, pp. 1-3.

Thomas, Ronald, *MMCP Synthesis*, Bardonia, New York: Media Materials Inc., 1971.

Lenore Pogonowski is Associate Professor of Education, Department of Music and Arts in Education, Teachers College, Columbia University.

The Jazz Experience in General Music

Bert Konowitz

The concern for active student involvement in the general music classroom appears to have become firmly rooted. It is becoming increasingly common for general music teachers to construct instructional designs which borrow bits and pieces from a variety of participatory-type approaches, including Orff, Dalcroze, Kodály, Improvisational Method, Manhattanville, and others. Many music educators feel it necessary to go beyond the listening-analysis experience and to experiment with an array of musical behaviors that enable students to test musical concepts in "real life" settings. These behaviors include composing, improvising, conducting, arranging and performing. Beyond engaging in a "lively experience," students who are learning to act, look and feel like musicians by doing musicianly things are gaining vital knowledge regarding the ways in which the musical elements function.

The Jazz experience is perfectly suited to this type of instructional need. The Jazz performer is intimately involved in a musical activity in which composing, improvising and arranging (organizing) comprise the performance. The Jazz performer usually begins by playing a given composition. Then, he or she must apply specific performance devices so that the appropriate stylistic flavor of Jazz is created. This is not a very creative activity at this point, for all the performer is doing is making small changes in the manner in which the accents, rhythms, articulation and phrases are used. In fact, it is appropriate to consider here that Jazz is a *way* of playing or singing.[1] Thus, small conceptual alterations create the sound, feeling and style known as Jazz.

Another aspect of Jazz is the creative one, where variational techniques are used to produce new melodic, rhythmic and harmonic patterns. Whether one takes only the first step (developing the Jazz style) or goes the full path and improvises, the process is a very exciting one. Imagine yourself as the composer/performer making split-second decisions that affect the use and development of melody, rhythm, harmony, dynamics, phrasing and articulation. What an exciting experience! And, what a terrifying experience! I have worked with many teachers who have had the courage to experience both the "terror" and the exultation, only to discover that their overall understanding and control of the musical language was far greater than they had imagined. Many of them also unexpectedly discovered that Jazz offered them a source for renewing their positive musical outlook and personal teaching energies.

There is a natural relationship between the general music classroom and the Jazz experience. A general music setting that seeks to broaden its base of participatory experiences to enable students to learn the musical language through firsthand activity is a most suitable place for students to work with Jazz. In spite of this obvious connection, many general music teachers are reluctant to use Jazz activity in their classrooms. This reluctance is often related to a feeling of being ill-equipped to deal with the "feel" and style of Jazz. Some even suggest that Jazz experience requires a special talent. Nothing could be further from the truth. Many teachers I have worked with have faced this feeling of "incompetence" be learning some simple basic Jazz-flavored skills. As a result, a large number of them have gone on to use Jazz as an effective tool for increasing student participation in the general music classroom.

Here is a basic, simple practice approach for the "non-Jazz" general music teacher. With consistent repetition, this workout plan will help music educators to become more comfortable and competent with the sound, feeling and style of Jazz. Practice these steps in private at first, exaggerating every phase of the program.

Teacher Practice Program

GOAL: To get the "feel" of the Jazz style.
1. The Jazz style is created by accenting the 2nd and 4th counts in the measure.

    •Tap or Clap:

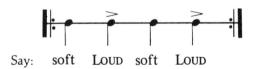

Say: soft   LOUD   soft   LOUD

    •Practice rhythms:

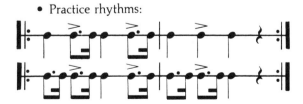

25

2. Scat words help to stimulate the appropriate Jazz sound (timbre).[2,3]
    •Say:

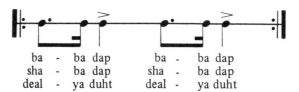

          ba - ba dap   ba - ba dap
          sha - ba dap   sha - ba dap
          deal - ya duht   deal - ya duht

    •Sing the following rhythms on random tone using scat words: (Note that in a
      syncopated unit, the sound of longest duration receives the accent.)

3. The blues scale is a fundamental component of Jazz melody.
    •Sing:

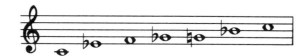

    •Using scat words, change the *rhythms order* of the tones (improvise).
    •Now record on a cassette player. Check appropriate accents, scat words and
      melody variety.
    Do not expect a miracle to occur: You may feel, look or sound like a Jazz "great." Yet,
continuing practice, you will feel the energy and excitement of creating.
    The ideas above can be transferred to the general music classroom. Following are
guides for planning such lessons.

AT THE SECONDARY LEVEL...
    GOAL: By clapping, speaking, singing, playing and improvising with the elements of
Jazz, the student will develop concepts of pitch, duration and structure.

26

Jazz Accents

Begin by having the entire class clap the playback; then have smaller groups and, finally, individuals respond. Assign individual students to dictate patterns to the class.

•Teacher claps:

•Students answer:

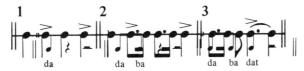

Scat Talk (Jazz sound). Move from entire class to small group to individual response. Later, develop new rhythms, emphasizing accents on "2" and "4."

•Teacher speaks:

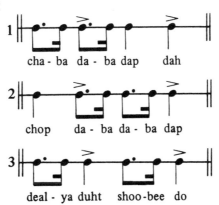

•Students answer:

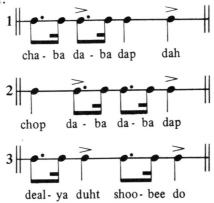

Jazz Melody

•Teach the blues scale:

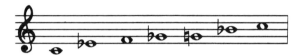

•Use the following rhythms to sing the blues scale (with scat words), changing the order and direction of tones:

•Teach the blues harmonic progression with students performing on bells and keyboard instruments:

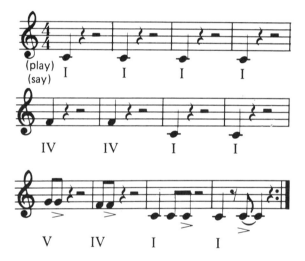

Jazz Organizing and Improvising

•Choose a student conductor to lead the class in performance of the blues progression. Emphasize changes in dynamics and instruments.
•Add solo improvisors to scat sing on the blues scale as class continues blues progression.
•Present a recording of "In the House Blues" sung by Bessie Smith. (*The Story of the Blues,* Columbia Records, G 30540.) Discuss Jazz style, sound and techniques.
•Divide class into small groups to create improvisations. Students may add words, devise new instruments, extend performing ability on traditional instruments by improvising, or add movement.

The approaches outlined above offer many extension opportunities. Reading about the places, people and settings that comprise the past and living history of Jazz offers students a unique view of the social history of America. The very short discography at the conclusion of this article offers some tools for adding aural reinforcement to the creative activity.

Jazz pervades the musical scene today, from the TV commercial to movie film scores to the most austere and distinguished concert hall settings. This broad musical presence offers the general music teacher an opportunity to connect the real world of the student to abstract musical concepts through the experience of creating. Experiential learning looms as a very necessary aspect of a student's education in an environment where the individual is increasingly losing personal control over the daily events of life. Jazz experience in the general music class is a good means by which to counteract that trend.

Selected Discography

Folkways Jazz Series, Volumes I-XI.

History of Classic Jazz, Volumes 1-10. Riverside Records SDP-11.

The Smithsonian Collection of Classic Jazz, Division of Performing Arts, Smithsonian Institute, Washington, D.C. 20560.

References

[1] Konowitz, Bert, *Jazz Classroom Activities.* Plans Ahead, Inc., 12 Hemlock Dr., Syosset, N.Y.

[2] Fredrickson, Scott, *Scat Singing Method.* Scott Music Pub. (Distr. by Alfred Pub. Co.)

[3] Konowitz, Bert, *Vocal Improvisation Method.* Alfred Publishing Co., Sherman Oaks, CA.

Bert Konowitz teaches the Jazz Improvisation and Popular Music courses at Teachers College, Columbia University and is Director of Music of the Lawrence Public Schools, New York.

SECTION THREE

AURAL EXPERIENCES

Eye or Ear: Which Route to Music?

Alice Parker

There it is, that elusive goal—**music**—shining on top of the far hill. How do we get there? Can the journey be pleasant? Should we *all* be on this trip?

Let us look at what we are doing in the largest possible context. Music has been around as long as human beings, and sounds from nature for millenia before that. The miracle of sound (and of the messages our other senses receive) is close to the central mystery of existence: our very bodies developed in answer to these imperatives.

Why, then, does our educational process not concentrate on the arts? Why do we not begin with a total focus on what our senses tell us, and with the crafts that result from that exploration? "Our job is to teach people to *think*," I can hear someone say; yct surely "thinking" is making "connections" that come only *after* sensory experience, not before, or without.

We have come a long way from our preliterate, unmechanized ancestors. When music, dance, visual arts, costume, feast and worship were one, it was within a world view that saw man and his "arts" as part of a vast whole. Think how we have since narrowed our vision. Music is now a "performing art," with entertainment its goal. Progress is defined as complexity, with a high priority on novelty. Printed music seems to tell us that only what the eye sees, can the ear hear.

Printed music—there's the problem. If we confine our music teaching to what can be notated, what are we losing? Is *pitch* what can be played on the piano with corresponding lines and spaces on the staff? Or is it a cosmos of vibration, and musical intonation the expressive use of that cosmos? (Remember that an electronic tuner finds one hundred degrees, or cents, between what we call "c" and "c#.") Is *rhythm* "a quarter-note equals two eighths," or "a quarter-note equals MM.60"? Or, rather, is it a play in time, based on the movement of our bodies in dance and our tongues in speech? Is form determined by formula, or by counting measures? Or is it what happens when a tree grows from seed, following its own inexorable laws? Do we hunt for these laws? Or think we can make up our own...

The trouble with music in the schools, I think, arises from our trying to put together a course of study which can be graded and tested (by written test, of course.) The page is an integral part of such a system, but music exists on another plane altogether. For me, as a composer, the page is a constant battleground. I hear living sound in my head, and can notate only about ten percent of it: all the subtleties of articulation, tempo and mood which make music live, defy the page. They can leap from the page to the experienced ear-and-eye, which hears the sound of which the page is but symbol. To the "literal ear" (a contradiction in terms) the page indicates a poverty-stricken music indeed, whose only "test" is accuracy to the written symbol. Anathema, to this composer, at least!

So what can we teach? SOUND. And how do we teach it? BY EAR, with the voice as test. Our goal should be training ears to listen and voices to sing. (Not vocal lessons, technique-en-masse, which can so easily desensitize the ear, but *song* lessons.) We should be filling young memories with melodies: singing all kinds of tunes without accompaniment, with communicative warmth and style and clear idiomatic uses of intonation, "beat," and diction. The teacher must be a role-model, able to sing convincingly in many styles; able to hear and reproduce those subtleties which make music "live," and able to teach the class to do likewise.

The feedback from the student should be song. The making of vocal sound, the response to mood and style, the ability to imitate, should all be considered of more importance than bald accuracy. Ease of response is what we're after, and that comes from years of experience in making music. The challenge here is to the teacher-as-musician, not as talker-about-music. It doesn't matter what kind of voice the leader has if the singing is engaging, that is, if it invites and encourages participation. The kind and quality of classroom equipment is secondary to a large fund of memorized songs. And keyboard, reading, and musicological skills are useful only if you can inspire, without them, a roomful or people to sound, and, yes, silence.

What's the bottom line? You cannot test musical knowledge verbally: that's "about" music. You can only test in terms of sound. How do you answer these questions?

How many songs do your students know "by heart"? (I love that expression.)
Do they sound musical?
How well can individual students imitate a new song?
Do students contribute new songs?
How freely can they improvise a setting, or hold their part in a round?
Does the class *love* its music-making?

Now, the perennial question: Where does music reading enter in? I agree with the Suzuki philosophy that it comes only after much hearing, singing and playing, and it amuses me to see how often we try to "improve" the system by starting earlier. It's like teaching cooking by learning to read recipes before you've tasted any food. (Is *that* how the cafeterias do it?) My theory is that *writing* should be taught before reading, and only after many and varied experiences in music making. But that's another article.

We can approach this whole process from another angle. Music is the most social of the arts. As opposed to the privacy of the page or the painting, music can unify a group of people in seconds, and it seems to be that that is one of its chief functions. When we are singing together we are communicating on a level far deeper than words. Our ears are connected to our minds and hearts in ways that defy analysis. Music *touches* us, and in so doing, civilizes us, socializes us, teaches cultural history and values, breaks down the walls between us, teaches us to concentrate on the "now" in a way that cleanses us from past and future worry, from the ceaseless agitation of our rational minds. If the classroom is a microcosm of society, can we not, through music, teach the human values our society so sorely needs—respect for quiet, for others, for working together; and the joy of creating something as a group that can't be done separately?

How do we open the door to this inestimable boon? If we take the page route, we are training eyes and rational minds, at the expense of ear and intuitive learning. Surely that's the long way around. Let us teach *sound,* and make music wherever we go. The benefits are both immediate and long-lasting—for students *and* teachers.

Bon voyage!

Alice Parker, composer-conductor, is a graduate of Smith College and the Juilliard School of Music, with an honorary doctorate from Hamilton College. Her musical activities take her all over the United States, and her music is sung around the world.

Four Strategies for Music Listening

Elayne Metz

'Turkish March' from 'The Ruins of Athens'
Ludwig van Beethoven

Beethoven was asked to write music for a play that was written for the opening of a new theater in Hungary in 1811. The play was about the history of Hungary and included sections about the Turks, who controlled Hungary at one time in its history.

For his Turkish march, Beethoven imitated the music—known as Janizary music—of the military bodyguards of Turkish rulers. The typical instruments of the Janizary were big drums, cymbals, triangles, and a fancy percussion instrument known as the 'crescent.' The guards must have presented a fantastic sight holding this long pole with a moon shaped brass plate on top, from which hung many little bells! It was played by tapping the pole on the ground while marching next to the ruler.

What instrument of a modern percussion section do you think best imitates the sound of the crescent?

Part of the Turkish flavor of the melody comes from the grace notes that Beethoven scattered throughout the piece:

Make your own Janizary music. Collect the largest drum you can find (to be played with a soft mallet), a triangle, a set of cymbals, and a tambourine to imitate the sound of the crescent. Practice the rhythm pattern below.

What dynamics will your accompaniment be? Why?

Section 1

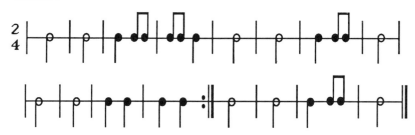

Section 2

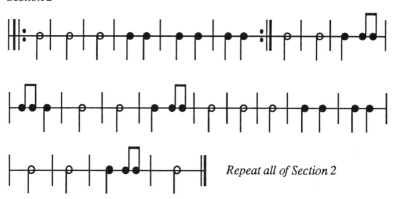

Repeat all of Section 2

Section 3

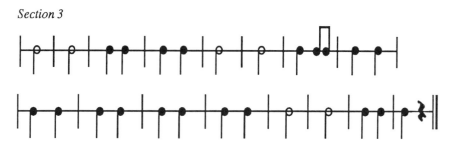

Now your Janizary band is ready to accompany the record.

'Simple Gifts' from Appalachian Spring
Aaron Copland

In the 1700's a religious group, whose meetings included shaking, shouting and dancing, settled in New England. They came to be known as the 'Shakers'.

One of their songs was made famous by the American composer Aaron Copland, who used it as a theme in his ballet *Appalachian Spring*. In the ballet a farm community celebrates the marriage of a young couple. Copland wrote the part of the bride for the famous American dancer, Martha Graham.

Copland composed a set of variations for this tune.

As a class, list on the board the ways a composer might change or vary a tune. Remember that when something is varied, it is possible to recognize the original version.

Listen to the recording with a paper and pencil in front of you, writing the number of each variation down the left side of your paper. Allow one line for each variation. Use the terms you have listed on the board to describe how each variation has changed. If you hear a change that was not listed on the board, write that on the line also. Discuss your discoveries with the class.

After singing the tune 'Simple Gifts' you may want to play an accompaniment on the bells. Below the song are samples of patterns you might play on the metal instruments, giving the effect of the chimes that are in one of Copland's variations.

Verse:

'Tis a gift to be simple, 'tis a gift to be free.
'Tis a gift to know just where you want to be.
And when you find yourself in the place just right,
'Twill be in the valley of love and delight.

Chorus:

When true simplicity is gained
To greet all as friend we shan't be ashamed.
To turn, turn will be our delight,
Till by turning, turning we come 'round right.

bass
metallophone

soprano
glockenspiel

alto
glockenspiel

'Les Toreadors' from 'Carmen'
Georges Bizet

Although Bizet was French, his use of realistic Spanish rhythms and dances gives the opera *Carmen* all the flavor of Spain. The gypsy girl, Carmen, loves the town's favorite toreador, Escamillo. In preparation for the bullfight, the ceremonial procession moves through the streets toward the arena.

Listen to the excitement Bizet creates with his use of quick rhythms:

Now the music changes as the toreador Escamillo enters. His song shows what kind of character he is.

What musical elements does Bizet use to describe the Toreador?

Part of the melody of the Toreador Song is printed below:

Bizet describes Escamillo's character with more than melody. Listen to the accompaniment for more clues to his personality.

Bizet used this tune for a dramatic purpose in his opera. His genius combines the music's liveliness with the audience's fear that something terrible will happen to Carmen. Outside the arena a soldier named Don Jose is about to stab Carmen in a fit of jealousy because he cannot win her love. The excitement of the bullfight combined with the knowledge of Carmen's approaching death creates a memorable dramatic moment in opera history.

38

'Air on the G String' from Suite No. 3 in D major
J. S. Bach

In 1985 we celebrated Bach's 300th birthday. This German-born composer, who was a church organist and choirmaster, never traveled far from his hometown. Yet 300 years later his music is known to more people all over the world than that of any other composer.

Bach's *Air* is the second movement of a collection of dances composed for orchestra. This melody, written for just the strings of the orchestra, is more like a song without words to be sung by the violins. The lower string instruments accompany the melody.

Circle the word(s) that best describe the violin melody. Put a square around the word(s) that best describe the accompaniment:

smooth	higher pitches	regular pulse	long and short sounds
separated	equal note values	lower pitches	louder softer

In Bach's day, violinists rarely played on the G string. It was not until 1871 that a violinist rearranged the melody from the *Air* to be played on the G strong alone. His renamed piece has been a popular selection for virtuoso violinists since then.

The music below is similar to Bach's accompaniment. Notice the form.

How many sections does the piece contain? (The repeat signs show the end of a section.)

While listening to the recording and reading the music below, conduct the meter and count the number of measures in each section.

Now choose someone in the class to play the accompaniment on the piano while the class sings. You can also play this accompaniment on a resonator bells or handbells. Each person may select one or more of the pitches below:

F# G G# A A# B C D D# E F F# G G# A A# B
(Middle)

Follow the music and play when it is your turn. The challenge is to play the accompaniment while listening to the recording! You may need a conductor.

Postscript on Listening

Eleanor Opp uses performance as a springboard for creative music strategies. She encourages her students to listen for those parts (rhythm pattern, melodic motif, etc.) that they believe, with some practice, they could begin to reproduce with classroom instruments. This type of strategy provides students with a personal goal for repeated listenings. It also gives the teacher an opportunity to introduce or reinforce notational skills as the class prepares their own version of the listening example.

Elayne Metz is a member of the music faculty at Arizona State University West.

Listening:
When Does It Begin?

Barbara Porter

What comes to your mind when you think of a listening lesson? Certainly many of your thoughts bring warm memories of a special experience, a first awareness of a now-favorite work, a discovery of a new style or composer. Perhaps you remember pretending to play a instrument with the music.

Unfortunately, it is likely that some of the memories are less positive. You may remember trying unsuccessfully to sit still, daydreaming to pass the time, or watching the clock for the end of class. What was missing in these lessons? Why didn't you listen?

Certainly there are many possible answers to this question and many contributing factors. But the most important reason for students' failure to listen is that they simply don't know how.

It is our job to teach them how, and that job begins not when we intend to share a recording but on the first day they walk into our classrooms. It is the work we do from day to day that leads to solid listening skills. Each singing and moving experience must focus on conscious listening.

The elements of pitch and rhythm are easily understood by students when they are introduced sequentially. Students delight in trying to identify a familiar song by listening to its rhythm in isolation. Truly this is a primary listening experience. If you alter the rhythm of a single beat within the song, students can identify the change. This focuses their listening even more.

The following activity demonstrates this process:

When the class can identify 'Great House' as you clap its rhythm, tell them that you are going to clap it again but this time you will change one word.

> *Great big house in New Orleans*
> *Forty stories high;*
> *Every window in that house*
> *Filled with chicken pie.*

Change the rhythm of 'window' (eighth notes) to 'door' (quarter note). Ask the students to tell which word you changed. Then ask what the new word might be. Do this many times.

There are many opportunities in change the rhythm. Soon the students will want to create the changes.

The entire experience will focus the listening of the class. It will also prepare them to understand what you mean letter when you speak of variations.

Tempo and dynamics can be understood from the beginning and should be considered with each new song. Students become aware of their own musicality when they have a chance to participate in these choices. They will also be better able to accept variety in the masterworks you present.

Students should experience a wide variety of musical styles from day to day and have ample opportunities to understand the difference. With practice, students will be able to change the meter or the mode of a familiar simple song. If they have altered 'Are You Sleeping' by singing it in its relative minor mode, they will be better able to appreciate listening to the third movement of Mahler's Symphony #1.

A student who can read and identify *mi-re-do* and who has had opportunities to create *mi-re-do* ostinati with pentatonic melodies is likely to listen to the way Bizet did the same thing in 'Carillon' from L'Arlesienne Suite #1.

Movement to music, too, should be based upon clear understanding of the relationship between the two. It is important to select music that clearly emphasizes an element—pitch, rhythm, style, mood, or form—to which you wish your students to respond. The more obvious the example, the better will be the response.

All of this takes time. Listening is a skill and must be developed. When does listening begin? It begins at the moment when you first meet your students. It continues each time you meet them. Your students' listening skills will be directly related to the way you nurture their listening in each lesson.

Barbara Porter, of Seattle, Washington, is a public school music supervisor.

SECTION FOUR

LEARNING PERSPECTIVES

Three Views
of the Child

Mary Louise Serafin

It is unfortunate that none of us in the business of music education were present in France in 1800 when the greatest educational experiment of all time was conducted—by accident. The experiment was attended by all the scholars, teachers, and public officials of the day, and its nuances were fiercely debated everywhere, as they continue to be today. The "experiment" was that a young boy was left alone in the woods for perhaps a decade; from early childhood he was not only without education, but without any human contact whatsoever, perhaps under the most severe conditions of cultural deprivation of any man in history. He lived on roots, travelled on all fours, and survived the bitterest winters. In 1800, for unknown reasons, he turned himself in at a small French village, and from that day forward he was attended and debated by all the leading philosophers, physicians, and pedagogues in France. They flocked to the rescue of this adolescent wild boy. Though he was dazed, mute, smelly, and surly, here at last was man in the raw, man in his natural state untainted by social influence. A thousand questions burst forth. Would the boy, in his isolation, have developed a language? Would the boy be possessed of any *ideas*? Would he have any emotions or a sense of fairness or affection toward others? Would he—one of us might have asked—have any aesthetic sensibility or even a spark of music?

To these questions the evidence answered "no," so badly had the experiment treated the boy. On the surface of it, he appeared hopelessly lacking in everything human, and resisted even the notion of clothing. Still, the experiment was not over: *Could* the boy be educated? Did early deprivation leave such a scar that no training now would help? Most important, if education were possible, what methods would be best? Had any of us been there, we might have asked too whether the joys of music and sound would forever escape this child savage.

The story of Victor is fully told in Harlan Lane's book, *The Wild Boy of Aveyron.* (Harvard University Press, Cambridge, Mass., 1979) He underwent his lessons; he died in 1828; he moved the course of thought on education and the nature of children forward a bit. But more important, the questions that Victor brought with him from the forest are the same ones that teachers face with every American child—wild or no: What is the nature of the child's development? How does learning *go*? Though the debate on such matters shows no sign of subsiding, teachers act out their own implicit answers, as they must, with their every entry into the classroom. Because the answers to such questions are so important, I want to sketch out the three general and conflicting answers that have dominated the debate since the time of Victor and before. Every reader, I am sure, will find a bit of himself in one of these three answers.

Consider the question: How does the child develop into an adult?

Children as Flowers

One answer to the question is that the child grows naturally, on his own, much as a flower grows from a seed. In this view the child requires little care beyond a healthy and stimulating environment, for everything that he will become is contained within him from the beginning. Seeds need water and care, but the "flower-ness" that they will later radiate does not need special attention. The view that children contain *within them* their own good seeds of adulthood is one that has been called the *innatist* or *maturationist* view. It emphasizes that growth comes from within, not from outside the child, and it stipulates that hard or forced learning from without may be harmful, at best useless. Just as a flower cannot be forced to grow, neither can the child.

The innatist view of children has old philosophical roots that had important ramifications in education. When Froebel invented the preschool program for children he viewed as flowers, it is no accident he called it "kindergarten." Teachers who subscribe to this view of children believe that it is the child himself, not the environment or the specific classroom activities, that controls the learning. Such teachers are apt to see themselves as sideline guides, but not directors. They are likely to emphasize unstructured learning, freedom, and self-discovery. In music, perhaps they would provide only materials and instruments and a warm and accepting atmosphere. With time, music would flower.

Children as Mirrors

An opposite point of view is taken by teachers and scholars in the *environmentalist* or *behaviorist* tradition. According to this view the child contains little or nothing in the way of seeds that will sprout themselves later. Rather, the child is as empty as a blank slate or even a mirror: He reflects only what is ground into him by the environment—no more, no less. The source of growth is not internal, within the child himself, but rather external, in the people and events in the environment. The child is the receiver rather than generator of his knowledge. Teachers who subscribe to this view focus on the environment more than the child, and they are concerned with structuring the learning environment in highly specific ways: They do not just provide materials and freedom, but they break down information into small bits; they build up knowledge step by step; they teach through imitation and repetition, with a clear distinction between right and wrong, and with rewards (and punishments) accorded respectively. In this view the teacher is not a guide who stands aside until needed, but rather a director who leads the way.

The innatists and environmentalists have been arguing such views for generations. Imagine the buzzing in the salons of France when Victor was discovered. The seeds of Victor's language, some would have said, were already contained within him, and he would need only a supportive, talkative human environment for them to unfold. No, the others would argue, language comes about only from a structured learning—the careful, step-by-step practice of small bits, words built up one at a time.

What might we have argued about music?

Interactionism

A third view of the developing child has been termed *interactionism* because it emphasizes not solely the child *or* the environment, but the interaction between the two. My model for this view is far less glamorous than either the beautiful flower or the clean mirror. Here the child is like an ordinary rubber band: Depending on the environment it can be stretched to great limits, but only so far; left to its own devices, it goes its own way. Teachers who subscribe to this view (which is most closely associated with Piaget) are careful about fitting the environment to the child. That is, they are convinced that only certain topics are appropriate at certain ages or stages of development, and they spend considerable energy trying to engineer the right match. They are also convinced, however, that once the learning materials have been aimed at the right level, it is up to the child to generate his own learning. Thus, such teachers might carefully design music activities and materials, but they allow experimentation and self-direction. Their role is neither the passive guide nor active director, but rather the instigator of children's learning. They use the child's own interests and creative impulses to build toward later learnings.

It is impossible to overemphasize the influence that these views have had, ancient as they are, on American public education and on music education in particular. It is only a slight simplification to say that traditional elementary and secondary education has been in the environmentalist tradition, whereas early childhood education has grown from maturationist roots. In music education, the interactionist view is only recently being developed.

My personal conviction is that the interactionist model has been best confirmed by research and is the most appropriate for public education. Our classrooms are peppered with Victors, both large and small, and they are neither flowers nor mirrors, but rather rubber bands: They are stretchable, limited, and surely holding their own forms.

Mary Louise Serafin is Lecturer, Department of Psychology, Yale University.

Setting the Environment for Aesthetic Experience

Margaret S. Woods

A POTENTIAL lies smouldering...

Fanned by the flickering flames of wonder and insatiable curiosity, the emerging light of discovery casts an eternal glow of fulfillment in the heart and mind of a child.

The human being at birth, with unknown potential for becoming more fully human, tunes into the world—listening and learning, observing and learning, thinking and learning, valuing and learning—always with the whole self involved in each experience. Every individual, when free to do so, adjusts to the environment to meet an immediate need.

If we keep in mind Walter de la Mare's criterion that "only the rarest kind of best can be good enough for the young," we will strive to establish an environment (physical and psychological) which will nurture compassion for all living things, responsiveness to and respect for others, and an inner sensitivity so necessary for creative, productive living. Such an environment will awaken in children imaginative responses to aural, visual and kinesthetic beauty around them.

A very aggressive child, visiting the Children's World at the New York World's Fair, held a kitten for the first time. "Listen," he said, "he's singing to me. How does he know how to sing? Where does he turn the singing on?" After holding the kitten for a short time, the boy commented, "I didn't know they were that soft."

The boy's physical and psychological climate allowed and encouraged

47

his aural and kinesthetic discoveries. His inner sensitivity was being awakened. Feelings were emerging that, with time and encouragement, might alter his total behavior.

What constitutes a psychological climate that will nurture the creative spirit and being about aesthetic growth? Here are some ideas:

1. Develop a capacity to care about all children. Remove barriers of race, color, or creed, so as to promote in each child a feeling of personal worth.

2. Create a restful atmosphere by being relaxed.

3. Allow wonder to permeate the classroom atmosphere.

4. Encourage and appreciate the imaginative expressions of children, accepting and subtly refining when necessary.

5. Develop a keen sensitivity to the minute, myriad changes in children, deepening and widening channels for expression when signals are given.

6. Keep space in your garden for "late bloomers."

7. Be ready at all times to participate as an eager learner.

8. Have fun. Support the child's feeling that the serious business of make-believe is in essence the "joie de vivre." Recognize make-believe as a potent source of courage and self-confidence.

9. Be aware of, and develop in children, an appreciation for change. For example, look for the fist signs of fall, winter, spring and summer.

10. Regard the unknown as an invitation to discovery, prior to and following any meaningful learning experience.

11. "Fence in" the pasture of creativity. Utilize limits which facilitate rather than discourage verbal communication.

12. Provide for practice in handling freedom with accompanying personal responsibility.

13. Work toward goals, but be more interested in the growth that takes place than in results that accrue.

14. Encourage evaluative comments, using them sparingly, but positively.

15. Include in your working vocabulary mysterious and magical words such as *hunch, intuition, make-believe, delight, compassion, courage,* and *faith,* and constructions such as *What if...?* and *Just suppose...*

As a rose in a suitable environment takes four days to emerge into full bloom, so a child, in time, will blossom in an environment designed to foster aesthetic growth. This is our challenge as teachers—to create Classroom Climate Control.

Margaret S. Woods is professor emeritus, Seattle Pacific University, Seattle, Washington. She is currently a member of the World University Roundtable.

SECTION FIVE

YOUTH MUSIC

The Sounds of America's Youth

Roxanne Metz

FOREWORD

When I engage adolescents informally in conversation about music, the ensuing discussion often provides a surprising amount of information useful to a general music teacher. In going beyond the expected, defensive "our-music, your-music" teenager-to-adult talk, I frequently find a dazzling array of superstars and their characteristic sound/apparels paraded before me, described as richly with aural and visual cues as any college music course lecture.

Teenagers talk a lot among themselves about music. In order to communicate what they like and whom they like among the current subcultures of youth music, they need to acquire sophisticated descriptive skills. Strengths or weaknesses in labeling timbres, textures or timbales become readily apparent. By listening, I glean an idea for a new strategy or two.

The following article, written last spring, reflects the views of an articulate teenage friend who has been patiently helping me to understand some of the current popular styles. This is her report.
(Jackie Boswell, Professor of Music Education, Arizona State University, Tempe.)

Madonna, Huey Lewis, Motley Crue, Prince, U2, Duran Duran. What's the difference? For teenagers, it is easy to tell the difference between the groups because we have been listening to this music for a long time. We have formed our own opinions on which groups are good, which are bad, and what kinds of sounds we like to listen to. For you, it may take a lot of hours of listening to decide if you like any of the sounds we teens listen to. Teenagers decide what kind of music they like, and they usually get friends with the same tastes. Groups get formed and names are formed like breakers, punkers, mods, etc. Rivalry occurs sometimes when groups of kids think that they are right and everybody else is wrong.

Kids decide what kinds of music groups they like by listening for the lyrics, instrumentation, how fast the beat is, talent, and if the singers are male or female. Teenagers look at the way group musicians wear their hair, and how many magazines the group has been in recently. To each individual, some things are more important than others. All of the factors are added up in each person's mind and then he/she can come to a decision about what style of music he/she likes.

In this article, I will try to help you understand the different groups, and what the kids are like that listen to the different styles. You must not look down on us kids because of the music we listen to, or because of the way we dress unless you have looked at us objectively as people and not just as kids with stupid ideas. The kids under the leather, the metal, the unmatching clothes that hang off the shoulders, the shaved hair, the colored hair, the bleached hair, and the hair that hangs in their eyes are really neat to me. They are putting up a wall between their generation and others' because it is easier not to communicate with adults and because the two generations do not understand each other. Another reason that they make this wall is because they like to freak out their overprotective and bossy parents, teachers and other authority figures. They get a big kick out of having some control over adults.

The first style we will look at is **light rock**. This consists of light music without much, if any, percussion or electric guitar. Most light rock groups use a lot of pianos and keyboards. Their songs talk about love and about the feelings people have after couples break up. Usually kids listen to this kind of music when they are in a mellow mood. Adults like to listen to light rock music sometimes, so some kids listen to it to make their parents happy or proud of them. Most kids that listen to light rock music are dressed well and don't usually get into trouble. This doesn't mean they don't do bad things, they just don't get into trouble for it because they are supposedly respectable people. A good light rock group is Lionel Richie. He has an album out called *Can't Slow Down* which is pretty good. Chicago's new record *Chicago 17* is also good. Chicago has been around for awhile. It has been making music continuously, and its new sounds appeal to teenagers.

Rock is the type of stuff kids listen to on the radio and at school dances. It uses more percussion and electric guitar than light rock. Sometimes synthesizers are incorporated into the music. Usually rock music can be danced to. It has a faster beat than light rock. Some good rock groups are Bruce Springsteen and the Scorpions. I would suggest listening to the Scorpions' album *Love at First Sting* to get a good introduction to rock music.

Break dance music was popular about a year or two ago. Anybody who could do the moon walk was "cool." Break dance music is filled with synthesizers. It is basically made up of rhythm and a lot of raps (rhymed chatter to the beat of the music). The music makes you just want to get up and move. Break dancing has been popular in the ghettos for years, but most people didn't catch on until a year or two ago. Break dancers wear bandanas, windbreakers, and sometimes leather jackets or leather pants because those kinds of clothes are easier to dance in than jeans. The jackets were worn so that when a breakdancer wanted to spin on his head, he would have a soft jacket for protection. Break dancing became unpopular shortly after it became popular. It came from the ghetto and went back to the ghetto. Midnight Star is a popular breakdance group, whose music is sometimes referred to as a technifunk style.

The next style we are going to look at is **heavy metal**. Usually there are no keyboards in heavy metal. Heavy metal has a fast rhythm. Most heavy metal groups are pretty talented. Heavy metal bands are showy and the musicians wear a lot of leather and chains. They have to look good and be able to play the music well to be popular. Most people who listen to heavy metal groups are guys who want to be in a heavy metal band when they grow up, and who can play guitar or percussion instruments. Heavy metal is not satanic. A lot of people think it is because of the clothes the musicians wear and the backward masking on records (messages disguised by recording backwards). All that it is, is just a big put-on to freak out adults and to make the kids feel "cool." Some good heavy metal bands are Van Halen and Iron Maiden. Iron Maiden has a very good bass electric guitar player, and he writes most of the songs, so kids who want to be guitarists listen to Iron Maiden.

Mod and **new wave** are two different styles, but I am going to mix them together because it is almost too hard to tell them apart. Mod/new wave music is full of synthesizers. That is mostly all it is—synthesizers and singing. Mod/new wave music originated in England, and is very popular there now. Most mod/new wave groups are made up of men. They talk about love, war, and abortion. Mod music is very mellow. New wave music is kind of fast and upbeat. This makes it sound like the two styles are totally different, but they really aren't. Mods wear rosaries and crosses, even though they might not be very religious at all. Both mods and new wavers wear big shirts and unmatching clothes. Mods like khaki and browns. New wavers like bright colors. Neither mod nor new wave clothes match. A good mod group to listen to is Depeche Mode. Their new album isn't that good, but it is popular. The old album *Construction Time Again* is about two years old, not very popular, but very good. Some good new wave groups are KajaGooGoo and Tears for Fears.

Punk is a hard style to describe to adults, because the idea that most adults have of punk is completely different than how it really is. Punk, like heavy metal, is not satanic. Punk came from the flower child generation when a whole bunch of students rebelled at Kent State University against the Vietnam War. Punkers and punk music talk about war, home life, school, and other things that kids think about. Punk music is meant for kids to let out their frustrations and anger. It doesn't take a lot of talent to be a popular punk group, but you have to be able to write good words. Most punk groups just play a couple of chords repeatedly, jump around, look silly, and shout their messages as loud as they can. (It's effective, isn't it?) Punkers (the people that listen to punk music) are usually quiet, sweet, and caring. When a whole bunch of punkers get together, they get rowdy, destructive, and loud. They do this to attract attention, to make a wall to cover up who they really are, and to freak people out so they won't try to get near to them. If people tried, they would find some really neat people. A good punk group is the Dead Kennedys.

I hope you understand teenagers and their music better now. It is very important that you understand our music and our point of view, especially since you are teachers and probably parents. After all, you have to understand us in order to communicate with us. Listen to some of the music. You might enjoy it.

Roxanne Metz is 15 and attends McClintock High School in Tempe, Arizona.

Teaching the Sounds of America's Youth

Timothy Gerber

Among the hundreds of general music students you teach, you're bound to find a few who know the answers to these important music trivia questions:

1. Who is the only musician ever nominated for the Nobel Peace Prize?
2. With which ensemble does this entertainer perform?
3. What is the name of the nominee's daughter?

If you already know that "Fifi Trixibelle" is the correct answer to the third question, you probably read the recent (August 29, 1985) *Rolling Stone* byline which proclaimed "The Boomtown Rat is Nominated for the Nobel Peace Prize." There's the answer to the second question. And as you may have heard, it is Bob Geldoff—leader of the Boomtown Rats—who has garnered three Nobel nominations. (One of these was submitted by the Prime Minister of Ireland!)

The name of Geldoff's daughter is truly insignificant trivia, but knowledge about Geldoff (his role in organizing the Live Aid concerts, the staggering $40 million in pledges these performances raised, and the resulting international focus on both pop music and world hunger) is not at all trivial for general music teachers. In fact, *caring* to know such information is an important theme in the accompanying article by Miss Metz. Caring to know is an attitude that is indispensable to general music teachers. Our abilities to converse about popular music sends students the message that we are interested in their musical passions. It provides a way to relate more personally to the youngsters we teach. And by listening to what is currently on the charts, we may discover some invigorating, refreshing music.

If you haven't done so already, you may want to examine the Live Aid performances. The recording of "We Are the World" has provided us with stimulating instructional opportunities for nearly all grade levels. Not only does the recorded tune present a veritable "Who's Who" in popular music, but it offers many opportunities for captivating lessons on form, harmonic structure, and popular vocal styles. (See the April, 1985 issue of *Life* magazine for good resource material.) And much like "We Shall Overcome," this song has invited literally thousands of people of all ages to sing together.

In addition to its musical import, much has been made of the sociological impact of the Live Aid concerts. As in the sixties, popular music and rock stars have focused our attention on larger issues. Unlike the Woodstock generation, however, the current Live Aid constituency has not been galvanized by the military draft or by anti-war protest. Herein lies a clue for understanding today's young people. They are, according to rock critic Pete Hamill, an "anesthetized" generation who "don't believe, as millions did in the sixties, that rock and roll could be a redemptive moral force, an agent of radical change. For them, rock & roll is not something fresh, original, special; it's the mainstream of American music. These are, after all, the first Americans whose parents grew up with rock & roll." (Pete Hamill, "A Day to Remember" in *Rolling Stone*, Issue No. 455, Aug. 29, 1985)

Miss Metz claims that it's easy for teenagers to differentiate among rock groups because "we have been listening to this music for a long time." Here Roxanne might have said that teenagers listen to this music continuously; her teachers more likely are the ones who have been listening for a long time—but not at all continuously. Perhaps that's part of the problem: general music teachers' rock listening habits tend to be sporadic.

Since sporadic pop listening habits probably prevail among the majority of general music teachers, we need to recognize one inevitable result: a clouded or non-existent awareness of the lyrics. As teachers, we need to know the exact lyrics and the messages they send. Popular music has always provided wings for adolescent fantasies; it offers a means of defining a particular generation and of thumbing noses at authorities. That's why each generation of teenagers cherishes forever the music of its own adolescence. Indeed, as Miss Metz has reminded us, the music provides a "big kick" in having some control over adults. This is a natural, and usually healthy part of growing up.

There is much in today's lyrics, however, that is far from healthy, especially when we consider its use in our general music classes. Since general music teachers have no control over what students hear and see on radio and TV and no authority over what music is added to personal collections of recordings, we must exercise informed judgment regarding the pop music we use for instruction. More than ever before, a deluge of trash is climbing the pop music charts.

More often than not, parents and teachers are unaware of the lyrical content of rock songs. Yet, listening to popular music and watching rock videos is imperative if we are to recognize the vulgarities in the lyrics our students know so well. Are you aware, for example, of the explicit indecencies in Prince's *Purple Rain*, an LP that has sold nearly 10 million copies? In the song "Darling Nikki," Prince sings:

"I knew a girl named Nikki,
I guess u could say she was a sex fiend;

I met her in a hotel lobby,
masturbating with a magazine."

Listen for yourself; if you don't own a copy, borrow it from one of your students. (Nearly half of my eighth grade general music students had added this gem to their collections by year's end!)

Even when the musical content has great personal appeal, we need to be careful. I like Foreigner's 1981 LP entitled *Foreigner 4* because it contains good examples of danceable hard rock. The tune "Urgent" is a good case in point: while it's a great dance tune, the veiled vulgarities have no place in a general music lesson. Among its lyrics, you'll hear these words:

"Your desire is insane,
You can't stop until you do it again;...
But I'm not lookin' for a love that will last
I know what I need and I need it fast."

The "light rock" groups identified by Roxanne offer fewer crudities, but not all of their tunes are respectable classroom fare. Consider the propriety of using Lionel Richie's "Penny Lover" in your sixth grade general music class:

"Nights warm and tender,
oh, lying next to you;
Girl, I surrender,
oh, what more can I do?"

Or how about "Stay the Night" on Chicago's 17th album? While the musicality of the tune is enormously inventive, I won't use it in the classroom because the chorus contains these lyrics:

"Stay the night,
there's room enough here to two;
Stay the night,
I'd like to spend it with you."

Obviously, evaluating lyrics for content and appropriateness has become a necessary habit for teachers—a critical part of the planning process. In this regard, I find it helpful when lyrics are printed on the backs of album jackets.

Once we do identify those songs that are musically valuable and worthy of classroom use, our task is to focus on the music and its construction. As Roxanne has indicated, students may respond more immediately to the lyrics, the style and appearance of the group, or the popularity of the video version. Our job, however, is to help students develop the skills they need to identify and discuss intelligently the unique musical characteristics of a composition. When we do address the lyrics, it's important to do so in terms of the musical elements. Rather than asking what meaning the lyrics have for individual students, ask how the *music* either helps in or detracts from conveying these lyrics.

In preparing instructional strategies, I try not to downplay the importance my students attach to the lyrics. Instead, I focus on the musical appropriateness for the lyrics in question. Here are guidelines which may be of help.

1. Instead of using current hits, select another piece on the hit-song album. Chances

are good that your students will not know it well, so it will provide fresh material. Or wait a few months after the hit tune has fallen from the charts; students will enjoy hearing it again and may be better able to focus on your objectives.

2. Listen for compositional aspects that appear to be new. The increasing use of electronic instruments provides intriguing opportunities for discussion about timbre and texture. (Read *Keyboard* magazine to stay current with new instruments and reviews of related recordings.)

3. Screen the recordings your students bring to class voluntarily. Since we all have students who enjoy pulling the wool over our eyes, avoid embarrassment by borrowing and listening to your students' recordings prior to playing them in class.

4. As a general rule, avoid the use of rock videos in general music classes. Not only may they be too familiar to your students, but the visual material usually preempts a proper focus on musical content. (The vulgarity of some videos, particularly those that portray violence against women, are in my judgment among the ugliest elements in popular music today.)

5. Stay current with the rock scene in general and with your students' preferences in particular. Read *Billboard* and *Rolling Stone* occasionally. Talk with your students informally about their most recent record purchases. Listen to examples in each of the categories identified by Miss Metz. Even if you have a low tolerance for "heavy metal," it's helpful to know that Eddie Van Halen is one of the greatest guitar virtuosos in rock today.

6. Try to create performance opportunities derived from the music you select. Ask students to make judgments about which accompaniments they might create to support singing by the entire class. (I do *not* advocate singing the lyrics along with the recordings.) Notate the bass lines and play these on keyboards or mallet percussion. Tape record your in-class performances.

Finally, if we are to understand our students as Miss Metz has advised, it is helpful to remember that we frequently ask them to describe compositions by making informed musical judgments. The *only* time we as teachers may reasonably expect our students to listen attentively while solving musical problems is when we do the same thing. After all, attentive listening is really the first step in creating teaching strategies that pose the kinds of musical problems that enliven our students' learning process.

Most recently, I have found that Chicago, Huey Lewis, Stevie Wonder, Lionel Richie, Julian Lennon, Linda Ronstadt, Bruce Springsteen, Joe Sample, Aretha Franklin, and Billy Joel all have produced works appropriate for classroom use. The following strategies, developed with several groups of middle school students, have led to some highly enjoyable classroom experiences. Have fun with these ideas. Remember, rock & roll usually invites a certain *joie de vivre*!

Timothy Gerber is Assistant Professor of Music Education at The Ohio State University, Columbus. He also teaches eighth grade general music at Everett Middle School in Columbus.

SECTION SIX

SPECIAL EDUCATION

Partners For Learning Music Education— Special Education

Jack Kukuk

There is no doubt that music, as well as the other arts, plays a significant role in the perpetuation of a responsive and expressive citizenry. One of the functions of education, including arts education, is to help *each* person to achieve all he or she can. But this opportunity has not always been available, as Senator Kennedy so clearly stated at a conference at the Kennedy Center in 1974.

"It is difficult to admit to ourselves that for more than 150 years, we have excluded the mentally retarded from our society. We buried them alive in institutions where they were confined away from their families, their doctors and their friends. The talents and thoughts and skills that lay hidden within them were locked as well. Only now, and only slowly, have we begun to reverse that pattern and to recognize their rights to develop their potential."

Historical Perspective

Efforts to use music and the other arts in the education of handicapped students can be traced to the late eighteenth century. The works of several specialists in France, notably Jacob Rodriques Perier, Charles Michel, Abbe de l'Eppé, Jean Marc Gaspard, and Itard and Jean Esquirol provided that groundwork for those that were to follow. Edouard Sequin, drawing on work of those who had preceded him, brought these ideas and research into clear focus and provided the basis for techniques used in music education with special students.

Dr. Richard Graham, Professor of Music and Director of Music Therapy Programs at the University of Georgia, says of Sequin:

"Only a cursory review of Sequin's philosophy of teaching the retarded will bring to mind many of the methods, techniques, procedures, and systems that characterize ad underlie contemporary American music education...It is interesting to note that many respected educators have been directly influenced by Sequin, including Dalcroze and Montessori. Sequin, however, is the fountainhead of music education with exceptional children."

In the United States, some of the earliest reported programs of music were for the blind in New England in 1832. Other programs of music for institutionalized retarded persons were reported in the mid-nineteenth century, and by 1892 some type of music education was offered in all state institutions existing at that time. Sequin's influence was very strong, and his sequential-developmental methods have provided a basis for the music education programs not only for the handicapped, but for all children.

The inclusion of special programs for handicapped students in the public schools of the United States began as early as 1869. These programs have steadily broadened in scope and number since that time to a point where every school district must offer, or make provisions for, special programs for children with handicaps.

Public law 94-142, enacted in 1975, assured that students with handicaps have a right to a free appropriate education in the least restrictive environment. Furthermore, the law mandated that this "right" should be assured by the creation of an *individualized education program*" (I.E.P.) written specifically for the student. The potential within the I.E.P. for prescribing the arts as content and/or process is subject only to the boundaries of human vision. Full realization of such possibilities rests with school systems in which arts specialists, parents and special educators work and learn together.

Dr. Abraham Maslow, who was Professor of Psychology at Brandeis University and President of the American Psychological Association, spoke at the Tanglewood Symposium of Music in American Society (a gathering convened in 1967 by the Music Educators National Conference) of a new concept of learning, of teaching and of education. He said:

"...that the function of education, the goal of education—the human goal, the humanistic goal, the goal so far as human beings are concerned—is ultimately the self-actualization of a person, the becoming fully human, the development of the fullest height that the human species can stand up to or that the particular individual can attain."

"The arts are so close to our psychological and biological core, so close to this identity, this biological identity, that rather than think of these art courses as sort of whipped or luxury cream, *they must become basic experiences in education.* I mean that this kind of education can be a glimpse into the infinite, the ultimate values. This intrinsic education may very well have art education, music education and dance education as its core."

In recent years psychologists have addressed the levels of cognitive processing—how one processes data/information once it is received. Much is being said about the importance of education programs which call the learner to respond at the highest cognitive levels. If educators are to achieve "excellence in education" they must work toward a full range of cognitive responses—ability to name, understand, apply knowledge, analyze, create and make judgments.

In addition to providing for growth in cognitive responses, educators must assure that sensory-motor responses of learners also are functional. Special education programs have helped educators look more carefully at the receptive skills of students. Music learning requires high levels of receptive performance; thus, music is an important medium for developing auditory responses. Maximum musical growth cannot be achieved without careful attending, precise discrimination, sequential memory, perception of figure-ground relationship, closure and auditory motor integration. All of these are fundamental auditory processes.

A Case History

This story about Frank, a nine year old fourth grader, may provide some insight into the auditory learning process. In Frank's school district the instrumental music program was introduced at the fourth grade level. Frank, together with all fourth graders, went to the multi-purpose room where the band teacher played several instruments, talked about each instrument and invited the students to consider becoming a part of the beginning "band" class. Permission forms were distributed. Frank had liked the look and the sound of the trombone. It was fun to see how the slide changed the sound. Expectantly he carried the slip home to get his parents' permission signature.

Frank was a student with a learning disability and his parents were concerned about how the amount of time he would miss from his regular classroom might affect his general learning skills. Frank was fortunate. His parents made decisions based on all the information they could acquire. They, with Frank, went to consult the classroom teacher concerning the advisability of Frank's being out of the classroom for this additional time.

Frank's classroom teacher suggested that they all go to consult his learning disability teacher. A review of Frank's testing information indicated that the problem was clearly a case of impairment in the auditory channel; Frank could not effectively process information that he had heard. The L.D. teacher suggested that being involved in the instrumental program might very well have an impact on his learning problem, as playing the trombone was something he was highly motivated to do.

Frank and his parents, with the blessings of both the classroom teacher and the L.D. specialist, went to the music store, leased and later purchased a trombone. Frank joined the beginning class and his band teacher became an active, informed member of Frank's teaching team. Within six months Frank's ability to hear and process information had improved so dramatically that it was no longer necessary for him to work with the L.D. teacher. By the admission of all those concerned, music had played a vital role in Frank's progress.

A Team Approach

Music teachers can offer knowledge and skills to assist in the diagnosis of and prescription for students with auditory learning problems. The following list offers one taxonomy for observing receptive skill development in students.

1. Does the student *attend*? Is he/she able to listen for extended periods of time?
2. Is the student able to *discriminate*, to recognize likenesses and differences in sound?
3. Is the student's *auditory memory* functional? Can he/she recall something about that which has been heard?

4. Can the student *sequence* or *order a series of sounds*, recalling and performing patterns?
5. Does the student have *figure-ground* ability? Is he/she able to focus the listening on an element of sound in relation to other sounds heard simultaneously?
6. Can the student *associate sounds with symbols*?
7. Is the student's *auditory closure* functional? Is he/she aware of beginnings and endings?
8. Does the student have *auditory-motor integration*? Is he/she able to coordinate sound with movement?

Music teachers and special education teachers must become more intentional partners in the education of all children. Responses which are developed as necessary tools of musicianship are also fundamental tools for general learning. The general music teacher, upon observing a child's inability to perform effectively the tasks described above, should consult with the classroom teacher and special education teachers. By so doing, music teachers can play an important role in the diagnosis of learning problems.

Music teachers might also invite learning disability and classroom teachers to inform them of students who may be experiencing auditory learning problems; together they could work as a team to diagnose and prescribe learning activities for those students. A child who does not sing in tune may have a problem in auditory discrimination, auditory memory, auditory sequencing or in using the voice, a fine motor skill. The disabilities should be individually analyzed and, when identified, corrective measures prescribed.

Music educators have other allies in their efforts to serve students with disabilities. It is important to know of these groups in order to work toward the common goal of providing an equitable music and art program for all children. The National Committee, Arts with the Handicapped (NCAH), is a partner in this endeavor. Through its statewide network of Very Special Arts Festival (VSAF) programs, music educators are becoming an integral part of a range of activities which demonstrate the value of the arts in the lives of students with disabilities. The NCAH national office maintains a collection of curriculum and in-service training materials which can be ordered through its publication division. NCAH maintains a listing of consultants who are available for technical assistance and training in the area of music for students with disabilities. NCAH is an educational affiliate of the John F. Kennedy Center for the Performing Arts, Washington, D.C.

Jack Kukuk, a former music teacher, is Director of Education of the John F. Kennedy Center for the Performing Arts and is a member of the Board of the National Committee, Arts with the Handicapped.

SECTION SEVEN

GENERAL MUSIC PERFORMANCES

A Marketing Strategy for General Music

Karen Fitzpatrick

What did the audience *learn* at your last program? Programs provide opportunities to educate beyond the classroom—the parents, school administrators, the community at large, and most importantly, the children. As the goals, objectives, and teaching/learning processes of music education are made evident through public performances, we validate our role in basic education. Of course, our means and ends can be justified only in the light of *meaningful* curriculum.

Programs that are outgrowths of classroom instruction increase the availability of valuable time for regular classroom experiences. As programs develop on a day-to-day basis, incentives are created for children to raise their achievement levels, because they know there is opportunity for performance. This process enhances the total quality-control environment of the classroom. Creating a direct relationship between classroom experiences and programs allows children to share their authentic feelings about the beauty of music and the joy of creating it.

We need to work smarter, not harder, by making program preparation and performance an *integral* part of the curriculum, not an isolated element. The day-to-day activities and achievements of students in music should be as satisfying and important to them as the day-to-day A's and 100's of a math or language class. Programs need to represent more than final grades. As outgrowths of daily work, they can provide culminating experiences or being closure to units of study, thereby playing an important role in the total scheme of music education.

Programs that grow out of classroom experiences also provide opportunities for parents to see and hear the music learning and skill development that has taken place in the music class. Unlike other studies in which students take papers or projects home frequently, most musical achievements must be communicated through "live" performance. As children work through the process of producing music, they have numerous opportunities to develop self-confidence and poise in front of their peers and adults. Programs simply provide the final opportunity for students to demonstrate the confidence they've been gaining through frequent practice.

Another way to communicate classroom learning is to invite parents into the classroom for an informal program in which students demonstrate or perform for a small audience (such as students and staff members). These informal programs might consist of culminating activities from a unit of study, demonstrations of creating music, or performing polished products. Informal programs may be held during the school day and generally need not disrupt the normal flow of school activities. Informal programs also provide a setting conducive to dialogue between parents and the teacher.

Incorporating daily classroom experiences into formal (traditional) programming can result in the avoidance of the "puttin' on the style" syndrome, in which we use our best attire and manners to impress our guests. Of course, we should put our best foot forward at every program, but we might want to consider putting the *focus* on the musical experience and learning, rather than on the extra-musical "trimmings" frequently seen in formal performances.

Efforts need to be made to avoid planning programs in which the activities, rehearsals, and preparation of materials continually fall beyond the range of normal classroom preparation time. Such programs can cause disruption to the educational process of the entire school. When preparation involves other teachers and facilities, each person's role and responsibility needs to be clearly defined, understood, and supported by all who are involved.

There are many ways to help an audience better understand what is being heard during a performance. Why not turn to the audience and offer comments such as the following:

"Listen to this theme to be imitated at different pitches as each successive part enters." (Then sing or play the theme to which you refer.)

"You will notice that the composer uses this simple 5-tone melody in the form of a canon. In a canon several groups sing the same melody, but enter at different times to create a harmonic effect."

Such comments help the audience understand what is being heard and therefore increase the potential appreciation for music education. The comments also remind students of their musical learnings, not to mention the personal warmth that is brought to a performance when the director turns and speaks warmly and directly to the audience.

As our audiences become more aware of the goals and objectives of music education, both tangible and attitudinal support will be generated from parents, staff and community.

Through seeing programs that are derived from personal expression and meaningful musical experiences of the children, parent-teacher organizations will become more supportive of music education, perhaps even in financial ways. The kinds of programs in which the content is developed from sequential, meaningful music curriculum surely are preferable to superimposed, artificial-theme programs designed to tie randomly-selected materials together.

Let's begin thinking of programs as marketing strategies for general music. Let's give audiences the opportunity to participate in the music-making, whether as performer, listener, critic, composer, or director. Let's offer our audiences moments of personal, intangible, intimate satisfaction that are possible through the creative expression of music. It is the purpose of education to help people learn to think, to solve problems, and ultimately to improve the quality of their lives. Therefore, I suggest that the verbal, analytical, objective, measurable knowledge and skills are "not all there is." Those things are *part* of what makes for an improved quality of life. However, it is the intangibles—the attitudes, habits, understandings, and the ability to use tangibles—that allow us to make choices about the quality of our lives. It is evident that the two (tangibles and intangibles) need each other. Programs that reflect classroom learning provide excellent opportunities to communicate this need to our many audiences. It is the "doing" art or the "being moved" by an aesthetic experience that affects and improves life.

We *can* sing to full auditoriums. We *can* have standing room only. We *can* create programs that reflect the best of our classroom learning. We *can* raise the level of musical participation throughout the school. We *can* help others answer the question, "Is music basic?", if we can show the "why," "what," and "how" of our last program. Music and the arts *can* lead the curricular train, not the curricular caboose!

Karen Fitzpatrick is an assistant principal in Jefferson County Public Schools, Denver, Colorado, and is a former music specialist. Appreciation is expressed to Cherilyn Smith-Marble and Nancy Dunkin, music specialists in Jefferson County Public Schools, for their contributions toward this article.

Demonstrating General Music Learning in a Public Performance

Rosemary C. Watkins

Accountability in education may be a more critical issue today than it has even been before. All disciplines, including the fine arts, must show evidence of results.

Choral and instrumental performing organizations have an obvious forum, the public concert, for displaying student achievement in music. General music has no traditional means for presenting course content and student progress to the public.

The following scenario is intended to be a model by which the learning sequence of acquiring a musical skill or specific musical knowledge in a general music curriculum can be demonstrated publicly, i.e., at school "open houses," at parent-teacher organization meetings, or as a segment of a concert by school performing organizations.

The short "play" format can be adapted to any musical activity that is included in a general music curriculum.

A suggested procedure for writing dialogue is first to order all the steps that occur in a learning sequence. It is important to include the initial step of the learning process in order to highlight, for the audience, the difference between entry level skills and more advanced musical learnings. (Example: "In the beginning, we knew only one chord.") After writing the script in language appropriate for the grade level, have several students read the dialogue aloud to determine if revisions in style are necessary. An exact rendering of the dialogue is not as important as a natural style of delivery by students.

Mastering the Guitar

Instructional Sequence

Introduce
Strum a I (D) chord.
Accompany a one-chord song using I (D).
Suggested: "Are You Sleeping, Brother John?" or "Row, Row, Your Boat."

Reinforce/Introduce
Strum a I (D) chord and a V7 (A7) chord.

Introduce
Pluck the root of a I (D) chord and strum.
Pluck the root of a V7 (A7) chord and strum.

Reinforce/Introduce
Pluck the root of a I (D) chord and strum.
Pluck the alternate of a I (D) chord and strum.
Pluck the root of a V7 (A7) chord and strum.
Pluck the alternate of a V7 (A7) chord and strum.

Reinforce
Accompany a two-chord song using I (D) and V7 (A7).
Suggested: "Mary Ann"

SCENE: Students with guitars seated on stools or a section of choral risers.

STUDENT: "In the beginning, we knew only one chord." *(Student strums a D chord.)* "But we found we could get by using the one chord for a few songs we already knew." *(All students strum two introductory measures and sing.)*

STUDENT: "There are not too many songs that can be played with one chord, but with two chords"... *(Student strums a D chord, then an A7 chord)* "we are able to play many songs."

STUDENT: "At this time, we also learned about plucking the root of a chord and strumming the rest of the strings." *(Student plucks the root of a D chord and strums the remaining strings... Student plucks the root of an A7 chord and strums the remaining strings.)*

STUDENT: "When a chord is repeated, instead of plucking the root each time" *(student plucks the root of a D chord and strums, repeating the procedure twice):* "we add variety by plucking the alternate note—the fifth degree of the chord—and strumming." *(Student plucks the root of the D chord and strums, plucks the alternate of the D chord and strums. Student plucks the root of the A7 chord and strums, plucks the alternate of the A7 choral and strums. All students sing and accompany a two-chord song using D and A7.)*

STUDENT: "Two-chord songs kept up busy for awhile, but then we found out that there were hundreds, perhaps thousands of three-chord songs. Adding the third chord was a little difficult" *(Student plucks the root of the G chord and strums, student plucks the alternate of the G chord and strums.)* "but worth the effort. With the third chord, we found we could play folk songs—rock, country, blues... The list goes on and on."

Introduce

Pluck the root of a IV (G) chord and strum.
Pluck the alternate of a IV (G) chord and strum.

STUDENT: "At the time we learned the third chord, we changed our style of accompaniment. Remember the old pluck the root and strum technique?" *(Student plucks the root of a D chord and strums.)* "Now we are playing what is called a finger-picking pattern." *(Student plucks the root of the D chord and finger-picks strings 3, 2, 1.)*

Reinforce

Pluck the root of a I (D) chord and strum.

STUDENT: "With this new style of playing we can accompany singers and guitar solos." *(Students accompany a vocal or instrumental melody of a three-chord [D, G, A7] song in D. Students pluck the root [alternate] and finger-pick strings 3, 2, 1.)*

Introduce

Pluck the root of a I (D) chord and finger-pick strings 3, 2, 1.

STUDENT: "So far, we have played only major chords. But, one day we learned our first minor chord." *(Student plucks the root of the em chord and strums, student plucks the alternate of the em chord and strums.)*

Reinforce

Accompany a three-chord song using I (D), IV (G), V7 (A7).
Pluck the root (alternate if chord is repeated) and finger-pick strings 3, 2, 1.
Suggested: "This Land Is Your Land."

STUDENT: "Luckily, we found a few songs that can be played with only a minor chord." *(All students sing and accompany a song with the em chord. Students pluck the root [alternate] and strum.)*

Introduce

Pluck the root of a i (em) chord and strum.
Pluck the alternate of a i (em) chord and strum.

STUDENT: "The new minor chord helped us to play a different kind of music—folk songs of the Middle East." *(Students sing and accompany a folk song of this genre with the em chord, using a simple strum.)*

Reinforce

Accompany a one-chord song using a i (em) chord.
Strum for the root (alternate).
Suggested: "Hey, Ho, Nobody Home."

STUDENT: "We found that the guitar is not just for accompanying. The guitar is also used for playing melodies." *(Students play a melody in the key of G using open strings.)*

Reinforce
Accompany a one-chord song using a i (em) chord.
Strum from the root (alternate).
Suggested: "Shalom Chaverim" or "Zum Gali Gali."

Introduce
Play a melody using open strings.
Suggested: "Reveille"

Reinforce
Play a melody in G.
Accompany the melody using a I (G) chord.
Pluck the root (alternates and finger-pick strings 3, 2, 1.
Perform as a round.
Suggested: "Are You Sleeping, Brother John?" or "Row, Row, Row Your Boat"

STUDENT: "Learning to play melodies made it possible for us to play solos and accompany each other. Our final song will be one that we played first—except that now we will play the melody and a finger-picking pattern accompaniment as a round." *(Students play the melody. Students accompany the melody with a I (G) chord. Students pluck the root [alternate] and finger-pick strings 3, 2, 1)*

Rosemary C. Watkins is Assistant Professor of Music Education, Louisiana State University, Baton Rouge.

SECTION EIGHT

GENERAL MUSIC IN THE HIGH SCHOOL

"Music for Every Child, Every Child for Music"

Charles B. Fowler

For decades, amid slogans such as "Music for every child, every child for music" and "All the arts for all the children," many arts teachers have been content to reach just the talented, the gifted, and the already interested. Hypocrisy notwithstanding, music teachers who agree philosophically that music programs should serve all students have often in practice focused primarily on developing new generations of musicians and music teachers, leaving the education of the masses largely to chance. Music education, particularly at the secondary level, has been elitist. By and large, music teachers have not reached the general high school student nor have they wanted to.

That picture appears to be changing. As a music teacher in Texas recently stated, "If we say 'music is basic,' we must also say 'for everyone.' It's just like math." Arts educators know that if the arts are to survive the present educational reform movement, they must be considered basic. Only the basics are accorded the full educational resources of planning, development, staffing, materials, and most important, *time* within the school day. Only the basics are considered legitimate and necessary curricula. Only the basics flourish. But there is a catch. The basics, by definition, are areas of study that are important for *every* students. If music is basic, it must be essential for all.

We now have a number of states that consider the arts basic and require local school districts to act accordingly. States exercise control over arts instruction in public schools in a number of ways. Some require that a certain amount of instruction in the arts be offered in elementary and secondary schools. At present, forty-two states mandate such instruction, though mainly in visual arts and music. Only twelve states require that dance and/or theater be offered at the secondary level. Minnesota, for example, requires that all high schools in the state provide a minimum of two credit hours in music and two credit hours in visual arts with a minimum of 240 hours in each. This kind of requirement guarantees that schools provide a minimum number of arts courses, not that students must take them.

The accompanying table shows three other ways that states mandate the arts in public schooling. All twenty-two states shown now have graduation requirements in the arts. While Missouri has required one unit (one year) in fine arts (defined as either and *only* art or music) for graduation since 1960, most of these states have adopted these requirements during the past five years. Yet the requirements differ considerably in the demands they make on the individual high school student.

Two states require study of the fine arts for just those students who are college-bound or who are in the advanced academic program. Rhode Island requires these students to take half a unit of study in dance, drama, music or visual arts; Texas requires them to complete one unit of study in drama, music, or visual arts. These states have not established requirements in the arts for students in the general academic or vocational programs, those not intent on going to college.

Nonetheless, there is a good deal of interest, particularly in Texas, in creating new high school courses in music to meet this new requirement for advanced academic students. These students are not necessarily performers, so that they cannot or would not choose a performing group to earn this credit. Without other options in music, these students would be forced to earn the credit in drama or visual arts.

Deceptively, eleven of the states in the table require a specific number of credits in the fine arts or other subjects for high school graduation. These other subjects range from foreign languages and the humanities, to computer technology, forensics, and practical or applied arts (shop and home economics). Such requirements may have little or no effect on the arts. In Connecticut, for example, any music course may be used to fulfill the one-unit requirement. But so may any vocational course, which can include almost any course so designated by the local districts. Accordingly, few students are actually affected by the legislation, and no special arts offerings have been deemed necessary. Acting optimistically, the Connecticut State Department of Education has suggested curriculum development in the areas of related arts, American studies, humanities, and other disciplines, particularly social studies, that could encompass the arts.

In Idaho, a humanities requirement of two units (effective in 1987) and four units (effective in 1988) embraces the arts. The requirement states that the credits "may be from any of the following: fine arts (including performing classes), foreign language, or humanities." Study in humanities, the accrediting legislation states, "is to be considered as an integrated program of studies which will incorporate the interrelationship of art, music, world religions, architecture, science, philosophy, and literature." But the ruling permits a student to substitute two credits in practical arts (vocational, pre-vocational, or consumer homemaking) for humanities. Such a student could then conceivably complete the requirements by taking two credits in foreign language, avoiding the arts altogether. Perhaps it is for this reason that the Idaho State Department of Education is not recommending a new course in general music, but rather broadening the curriculum in the performance classes to include significant components in language and structure of music; skills in performing, creating, and listening; understanding music history; appreciation and evaluation of music. These classes satisfy the graduation requirement for humanities.

States With Graduation Requirements in the Arts

State	Number	Subject	State	Number	Subject
*Arkansas	½, eff. '87	Drama, Music, Visual Arts	*New Hampshire	½	Arts Education (Art, Music, Visual Arts, Dance, Drama)
California	1	Fine Arts (Creative Writing, Dance, Drama, Music, Visual Arts) or Foreign Language	New Mexico	½	Fine Arts (Visual Arts, Music, Dance, Drama), Practical Arts or Vocational Education
Connecticut	1	Arts (Dance, Drama, Music, Visual Arts) or Vocational Education	New Jersey	1	Fine Arts, Practical Arts or Performing Arts
*Florida	½	Fine Arts (Dance, Drama, Music, Visual Arts)	*New York	1, eff. '89	Dance, Drama, Music or Visual Arts
Georgia	1	Fine Arts (Dance, Drama, Music, Visual Arts), Vocational Education or Computer Technology	Oregon	1	Music, Visual Arts, Foreign Language or Vocational Education
Idaho	2, eff. '87 4, eff. '88	Fine Arts (Creative Writing, Dance, Drama, Music, Visual Arts), Foreign Language, or Humanities	Pennsylvania	2	Arts (Dance, Drama, Music, Visual Arts) or Humanities
Illinois	1	Art, Music, Foreign Language or Vocational Education	Rhode Island	½	For college-bound students only. Dance, Drama, Music or Visual Arts
Maine	1, eff. '88	Fine Arts (Visual Arts, Music, Drama) or Forensics	*South Dakota	½	Fine Arts (Dance, Drama, Music, Visual Arts)
*Maryland	1, eff. '88	Fine Arts (Dance, Drama, Music, Visual Arts)	Texas	1	For advanced academic program students only. Drama, Music or Visual Arts
*Missouri	1	Music or Visual Arts	*Utah	1½	Dance, Drama, Music or Visual Arts
			*Vermont	1	General Arts, Dance, Drama, Music or Visual Arts
*States that require some study of the fine arts by every high school student.			West Virginia	1	Music, Visual Arts or Applied Arts

This table is reproduced by permission from Arts, Education and the States: A Survey of State Education Policies *(Washington, D.C.: Council of Chief State School Officers, 1985), p. 23*

Similarly, Pennsylvania requires two credits in the arts or humanities, or both. In response, the Pennsylvania Department of Education has issued guidelines for local districts that suggest possible linkages between the arts and humanities. "A course in the arts has a humanities component when works in the arts are considered from the standpoint of philosophy, history, or values." And, conversely, "A course in the humanities has an arts component when works in the arts are studied, performed, and/or created in order to understand their concepts and principles." Guidelines suggest that existing arts or humanities courses can be given the other dimension; they also suggest a number of new courses. It's too early to see what effect these new regulations will have on the district level.

When you get down to it, there are only nine states (those that are starred) that now require every high school student to complete some study of the arts in order to graduate. Four of these states require a half unit and four require one unit, while Utah requires one-and-a-half units. But this is only the beginning of the differences.

Seven of nine states permit—encourage—students to fulfill the requirement through a comprehensive program of dance, drama, music, and/or visual arts. One state, Missouri, requires students to complete one credit in art and/or music; and one state, Arkansas, gives students the option of taking a half credit in one of three arts—drama, music, or visual arts. The effect of these requirements on the music program varies considerably from state to state.

In Florida, June Hinkley of the State Department of Education reports that many students are opting to take the requirement in chorus. Schools are offering students other performance options such as guitar and, in some high schools, beginning band classes. About half the schools in the state have opted to lengthen the school day from six to seven periods in order for students to incorporate all the additional academic requirements and still have time for electives. In schools that have retained the six-period day, students no longer have the time to participate in performing groups, which has traditionally permitted a perfection of performance skills. Bands and choruses in these schools are suffering.

New Hampshire's Department of Education is advocating a new general music course geared to the average, non-performing student, although students can meet the requirement by taking vocal and instrumental music, music appreciation, theory, and other courses.

In New York State, which has instituted a one-unit requirement in fine arts effective in 1989, the State Education Department has published a syllabus for a new course for high school students, "Music In Our Lives," that requires experiences in five areas: listening, performing, composing, using basic tool skills (reading, following a score, conducting, etc.), and developing a special-interest, independent project (approved topics include computer music, synthesizers, new technology, the relation between music and its sister arts, utilitarian uses of music, a musical career, film music, music and dance in history, a musical composition, etc.). Students graduating in 1989 will have the option of three- and five-unit sequences in music in order to qualify for a Regents' diploma with a musical emphasis. One requirement of these sequences is that they include knowledge development along with the option of skill development or participation in a major performing group.

Utah's State Board of Education requires twenty-four units for high school graduation, including one-and-a-half units in dance, drama, music, or visual arts. A core arts curriculum with components in all four arts is mandated in the schools, K-12. High school students must pass a competency test in the arts to qualify for graduation. Core options in music at the high school level are music appreciation, music theory, chorus, band, and orchestra.

Effective in 1988, Maryland will require high school students to complete one credit of work in fine arts. Local school districts must offer high school courses that conform to the state curricular framework. While the music framework is in draft form at present and subject to change, it specifies four major goals: to develop the ability to perceive and respond to music; to develop the ability to creatively organize musical idea and sounds; to develop an understanding of music as an essential aspect of history and human experience; and to develop the ability to make aesthetic judgments. The local school districts are responsible for developing music curricula that incorporate these goals.

As in most states, Maryland's goals permit school systems to determine their own courses, to use their own ingenuity and local resources in complying with the new graduation requirements. Proposed course outlines must be presented to the state for approval before such courses are eligible to count toward the credit requirement. Each school board in the state determines the core of mandated courses for graduation and those necessary to complete a sequence to qualify for special diplomas in certain academic areas, one of which is the arts. Courses must be made available in each high school to permit students to achieve an arts diploma if they choose to do so. But if no students sign up for these courses, they do not need to be offered.

Both Anne Arundel County Schools (Annapolis, MD) and Baltimore County Public Schools (Towson, MD) are meeting these new state requirements in music by broadening and modifying courses already offered and by adding other courses. Still, their differences show the latitude given to local districts.

Anne Arundel County high schools now offer band, chorus, guitar, and keyboard as well as a course called Current Music in Perspective, I and II (each a semester in length). Performance classes have been broadened to encompass the dimensions of creativity, history, culture, and the valuing of music. The proposed music sequence encompasses five courses: Music History, Music Theory, Music Theater, and Current Music in Perspective, I and II. The latter course is designed specifically for students who do not have a performance background. As currently planned, it will have units covering a wide range: words and music, Romanticism, Classicism, technology, innovations in music creation and performance, careers, various cultural influences on music, the creative process, music and related arts, etc.

Baltimore County high schools also offer a general high school music course designed for students who are not performance oriented. Called "Music Perspectives," the course takes a Great Books approach to the study of music. It develops an understanding of music concepts through the study of eleven examples of music style and content. The concepts are derived from studying masterworks by Bach, Mozart, Beethoven, Debussy, Stravinsky, Ives, Copland, and others, and by studying the background of the composer and the relevance of the composition to the listener. Resource tapes permit teachers to supplement this study with a broad range of musics, including popular and ethnic forms.

Performance classes in Baltimore County high schools have been injected with a general education component. Incorporated into these classes are two units from the Music Perspectives course. Since most of these same teachers are teaching this course, they know this material well and are growing to accept as a fact of life this new approach to teaching ensembles. These high schools also offer a music sequence, but it consists of four performance credits and one credit in music theory. Obviously, the state's new requirement can be met in a variety of ways.

Viewed collectively, these developments reveal a trend in a small but growing number of states to provide study opportunities in music to all students at the high school level. This trend represents a fundamental change in philosophy—a move from a highly specialized, performance-oriented music program focused on the few toward a broadened, more academic program serving the many. It balances the emphasis given to skill development with acquisition of knowledge. As music education becomes more broadly based and more egalitarian, so too does it establish its basic import. Singlehandedly, these changes elevate music to a new and higher status in American schooling. Educationally, the arts are simply more significant when they are presented as substantive studies for all.

Charles Fowler is the former editor of Music Educators Journal. *He is presently Education Editor of* Musical America.

The Unfinished Task

Paul R. Lehman

T he most important single need of the late 1980's in our profession is for the widespread expansion of general music into the high school. Why? Because it's so fundamental to the purpose of music education.

In 1984 the MENC National Executive Board adopted three goals: (1) By 1990 every student, K-12, shall have access to music instruction in school; (2) by 1990, every high school shall require at least one unit of credit in music, art, theater, or dance for graduation; and (3) by 1990, every college and university shall require at least one unit of credit in music, art, theater, or dance for admission.

There is one clear and unmistakable condition that must exist before any of these goals can be achieved. There must be ample opportunity for *every* student to study music at the high school level. None of the goals can be achieved without the significant expansion of general music offerings in the high school. Too often today there are no music courses whatever available to the general student. By "general student" I mean the student who for lack of interest, ability, or time, or for whatever reason, does not participate in the school's performing groups.

In most systems students are locked out of instrumental programs unless they begin study in the elementary school. Our best choral groups also require prerequisite study. As a result, the majority of high school students simply have no reasonable access to music. This situation, which is directly contrary to Goal 1, is not the fault of a conspiracy of school administrators; it's the fault of our own curriculum.

Goal 2 calls for all student to study the arts in high school. But this is just not possible unless we make available music courses for the general student. Music is the most popular of the arts. It is potentially the most easily accessible to the majority of students. It would be unthinkable to try to meet this requirement through courses in art, theater, and dance alone. Twenty-two states currently include the arts in some manner among their requirements for high school graduation, but we have an immense task ahead to provide the courses that will make the requirement sustainable.

Goal 3 calls for colleges to require the study of the arts for admission. This is simply not feasible until arts courses become generally available in high schools. Historically, high school graduation requirements and college admission requirements have moved hand-in-hand. Colleges cannot require things that schools don't offer.

The strengthening of general music in the high school should not take place at the expense of our performing groups. The bands, orchestras, and choruses in America's schools are the envy of the world. We can take great pride in what we've achieved in performance. We must not dilute this strength, but rather safeguard it and build upon it. The performance program and the general music program should be complementary, not conflicting.

Larger schools, of course, can offer a greater variety of music courses than small schools, but even in the smallest school there should be at least one non-performance offering, without prerequisites, available every year to every student, and it should be scheduled so as not to conflict with required single-section courses. There may be a sequence of two or even three courses, so that advanced study is possible, but there must always be something available to every student. And we should utilize the music, the media, and the technology of today, because kids won't participate in an outmoded program.

In every high school there is a sizeable student population that is already favorably disposed toward music and would welcome a chance to study it. This includes many students who are very much "into" music as an extracurricular activity. Some of them have dropped out of our performance programs because of other demands on their time or because they felt unchallenged. Some of them have their own performing groups. Some of them aren't interested in performance at all but simply enjoy music and would like to learn more about it.

The music program must reach a larger percentage of the student population. According to figures from the National Center for Educational Statistics, less than eleven per cent of the nation's high schools offer courses called general music, only twenty-five per cent offer music appreciation, and only thirty-five percent offer music theory or composition. The most distressing finding of all is that the total number of high school students enrolled in non-performance courses is less than two percent of the student body. And that figure is dropping. How can we claim that music is basic in the face of such numbers?

John Goodlad, who has studied the school curriculum probably more thoroughly than anyone else in recent years, has recommended that at least fifteen percent of the program of *every* high school student should be devoted to the arts, and another ten percent should be available for electives, which may include the arts. Unfortunately we can't capitalize on his support because we don't have the courses. Some say that they problem is lack of demand on the part of students rather than lack of interest on the part of teachers. My observation is that if teacher interest is present student demand will follow close behind.

The widespread interest we're witnessing in an arts requirement at the high school level represents an opportunity of historic dimensions. I believe that the main reason many school administrators fail to support strong music programs is that they themselves did not experience challenging, rewarding high-quality music programs when they were in school. Our nation cannot afford another generation lacking these experiences. Expanded general music in the high school gives us one more chance to reach the students who within a few years will themselves be our superintendents, our principals, and our classroom teachers. These students will serve on our school boards, on our city councils, and in our state legislatures. They will be our mayors and our governors. They will be the parents of the children in our schools. They will be the public. What attitude toward music will we leave them with? How will they respond when we seek their support for music programs for their children?

You and I owe it to all of our nation's young people to ensure that they have every opportunity to experience music in high school. This obligation is based primarily on the unparalleled and indisputable contribution of music to a rich and rewarding and satisfying life. Music exalts the human spirit. Music enhances the quality of life. Music is basic.

But our obligation has even broader roots than that. The more graduates who have had challenging and rewarding experiences in music throughout their school years, the easier to will be in the future to generate widespread support throughout the community for our programs. And the easier it is to generate support, the more graduates are likely to have challenging and rewarding experiences in music throughout their school years. That's the kind of cycle from which *everyone* emerges a winner.

Music first gained a foothold in the curriculum 150 years ago through the efforts of a few bold and imaginative pioneers who were unwilling to accept the reality of the moment and who visualized a broader curriculum. Instrumental music became an important part of the school program between World War I and World War II, again as a result of the work of strong-willed and creative individuals. Now it is time to finish the task. It is time to balance our programs as they ought to be balanced. Once again we need bold and imaginative pioneers. Let's finish the unfinished task.

Paul Lehman is Professor of Music Education and Associate Dean of the School of Music at the University of Michigan. He is also Vice President of Music Educators National Conference.

The Continuing Problem of High School Non-Performance Courses

Bennett Reimer

As American education, and music education along with it, begins its climb upward from the doldrums of the past dozen-or-so years, unfinished business waits to be dealt with. Among the many problems of music education still left unaddressed, let alone solved, the most glaring might well be that of high school courses for youngsters not in performance groups (and for those who perform as well).

Symptomatic of the mechanical, administrative nature of the present movement toward "reform," the response of music education to the need for improvement has been at the mechanical, administrative level. MENC's "Goals for 1990," for example, call for a music curriculum, K-12, that is "balanced, comprehensive, and sequential." A music course should be available each year in high schools. One Carnegie unit in the arts should be required for graduation for high school and for admission to college.

In themselves, these are excellent, responsible (and politically astute) aims. So what is the problem? The problem, or course, as with all such procedural changes being called for in education, is that they rest on quicksand. What does "balance" really mean in a music curriculum? "Comprehensive" in what sense or senses? How does one achieve a "sequential" program if one is not clear about a) what to sequence, and b) *how* to sequence? What would a music course (or courses) look like that would be worth a Carnegie unit of credit? The Goals stipulate that the credit could be in "one of the arts or two or more in combination." How would one choose, and how would one combine arts if that were the choice?

It is almost painful to raise questions such as these. "Oh no," one feels, "do we have to go through all this? Can't we just get to work and *do* something?" Well, sure, we could just start running around again, as is our tendency. We have long years of experience in thinking we can solve our problems by expending energy madly. But we must, as much as we hate to admit it, take seriously the old saying that we run around "like chickens with their heads cut off." We cut ourselves off from our heads—our capacity for wisdom—when we forget that unless we *understand* better what we want to achieve, we will never accomplish more than an *appearance* of achievement. We simply must, like it or not, continue our work of self-definition at deeper levels than the procedural if we are ever to fulfill our professional potentials maturely.

On the issue of high school courses we find ourselves in a double bind—practical and philosophical. At the practical level a host of problems besets us. We presently enroll less than two per cent of high school students in any non-performance music courses, and we sense that even *this* tiny percentage is too large for those whose odious duty it is to offer them. Of course, there are some high school performance directors who take such courses seriously, enjoy them, and give them their best shot. But there are many more who disdain them, are threatened by them because they have never been helped to learn how to deal with them, and regard them as an imposition on their time and energies for all the reasons we all know so well. Few teacher education programs offer a course specifically dealing with how to organize and teach high school non-performance courses (music, arts, humanities, etc.), and those that might want to do so would be hard-pressed to find someone able and willing to teach it, so neglected has it been in our minds and hearts. Other practical problems, too numerous and depressing to mention, crowd in.

At the philosophical level the can is chock full of worms. So devoted is our profession to musical performance as the be-all and end-all of musical teaching and learning that courses focusing on skills of impression are likely to be regarded as "merely" such. I make this comment not at the obvious level of performance requiring a special commitment that only a few students are willing to make, therefore leaving only the half-hearted for courses, but at a much more profound level of the nature of musical experience itself and the role of performance in both enhancing it and limiting it. This is not the place to address the issue: I raise it only as needing to be addressed if we are to do more than putter about high school music courses. How, exactly, do we want to influence the music experiences of students? How does performance do and *not* do this, whether in performance groups or in classes? To what extent do non-performance experiences of music require both "knowing how" and "knowing that?" To what extent are *performance* experiences of music dependent on either or both? Must both kinds of knowing be included if we are to produce what education must, finally, produce—"knowing *with*?" Lurking behind these questions is another: what is the role of production skills, including necessary notation skills, in the knowings of music we want all children to have, and to what degree is the answer to this question seen in clearest light when we think about high non-performance courses? In that light, what do we see more clearly about elementary and junior high general music learnings that might reach fruition in high school courses?

As should be evident by the nature of such questions, our approach to solving the ongoing problem of high school music courses will, sooner or later, be based on our values—our deepest, most well-grounded beliefs about that which matters about our subject, and how we can most effectively share that with our students. We have, indeed, made progress toward clarifying our values during the past twenty or so years, but we tend to forget that we must keep in close touch with them, continue to refine them, *use* them as the basis for our practical decisions. To the extent that our efforts to improve high school music courses are efforts to apply our deepest values, they are likely to reflect the best of us, whatever faults they may continue to have. I urge that our debate of this issue be as reflective, as wise as we can make it, so that solutions will be both practical and meaningful. But I urge it also because in the good solution to this particular problem we may well find some essential keys that can unlock identical problems at all levels and in all aspects of school music. We have a double opportunity here. It may be that addressing this biggest gap in the music education program will also be our best way to fill in profound gaps in our entire program. It is high time we give the issue of high school courses the priority it deserves.

Bennett Reimer is John W. Beattie Professor of Music Education at Northwestern University.

Teaching High School General Music through Performance

Hunter March

Music plays a pervasive role in the life of teenagers. It provides a background for work and study, entertainment at parties, and companionship during hours of idleness.

If teenagers are so strongly attracted to music, why aren't more of them enrolled in secondary school music programs? First of all, many teenagers fail to see much relevance between "school music" and "music." Few instrumental and choral directors help students transfer the knowledge and skills acquired in class and rehearsal to the music which most interests them and their peers.

Secondly, most senior high school students are not interested in participating in the traditional music organizations offered in secondary schools—band, choir, and orchestra. Many of them do not particularly care to devote long hours of rehearsal to perfecting a piece of music, nor do they care to participate in public performances, prepare for contests, or accept the regimentation required by performance organizations.

Although many high schools offer alternatives to performing organizations, these alternatives usually take the form of courses in music history and theory. Such courses are frequently intended for potential music majors and are therefore too musically and technically advanced for the average student.

A general music course is needed for senior high school students who are interested in acquiring musical skills and understanding, but who are not interested in performing organizations, music history, or music theory. This course must differ from the general music of the elementary and junior high school, yet provide opportunities for students to acquire musical skills through performing, listening, analyzing, and organizing music.

Singing has always been the performance medium used in general music. It is ideal in that it requires no capital outlay, no storage space, and is easily transported. But singing also has limitations. Not all students like to sing. Those who enjoy singing and excel at it are usually enrolled in choir and probably will not elect general music. This does not mean that singing should be eliminated from the high school general music class; instead, it suggests that singing should not be the only medium used for performance.

People of every age, not just adolescents, want to *make* music. They like to experiment with sound and want to learn to play instruments, especially keyboard and guitar. Unfortunately, few schools provide students such opportunities. A general music course taught through keyboard or guitar performance could fill this void and attract more students to the senior high school music program.

The principal advantage of such an approach is its potential for intrinsic motivation. The desire to play the instrument should be the factor which creates curiosity about lines and spaces, key signatures, meter signatures, modality, etc. Furthermore, the development of performance skills need not depend solely upon one's ability to interpret music notation. This does not mean that music reading skills are not important—it merely suggests that one should not have to be able to read music before one learns to play an instrument.

Teenagers seek instant gratification. They do not want to wait a year or two before they're "ready" to play "their" music, nor do they want to begin learning the instrument by playing drills or elementary tunes. They want to know that in the very near future they will be able to play their favorite songs.

An introduction to the instrument can be made by teaching the students to play two chords, the I and V^7 in the key of A or D on the guitar, or in the key of C on the keyboard. Students can also learn one or two accompaniment patterns. Using these skills they can accompany numerous songs harmonized with I and V^7, executing two different accompaniments. When appropriate, meter signatures, key signatures, new chords, and other music fundamentals should be introduced. Concepts should be reinforced through listening to and analyzing other musical examples.

Students can sing the melody while accompanying themselves on the instruments. As singers they may be a bit shy and self-conscious at first, but before long they become so involved with their instrumental performance that they forget about their singing voices.

Eventually most students will want to learn to play melodies. This provides the perfect opportunity to introduce notation. Nothing motivates students to learn notation more than the desire to play the melody of a popular piece.

Many students who have developed sophisticated aural skills will enroll in general music. These students will often be able to learn chord progressions to familiar songs by listening to recordings, though they usually will not be able to identify or notate them. Such aural skills should be encouraged. Too often aural skills are neglected in the rush to prepare *legitimate* musicians who learn music through notation. (Remember, music is sound and was passed from one generation to the next through sound long before notation was developed.)

An inventory of keyboard instruments and/or guitars is required to teach a course in general music through performance. Acquiring this inventory is not as difficult as it may seem at first. Many student guitars and electronic keyboards can be purchased for as little as $100 each. Providing instruments for the normal class size of fifteen to twenty students would cost the school system $1500 to $2000. Whether or not you are able to obtain this inventory for your class may depend to some degree upon your ability to convince the administration that the instruments are necessary and the cost per student is not prohibitive.

Compare the cost of fifteen to twenty keyboards or guitars to the price of one student bassoon. A good student bassoon for use in band and/or orchestra could be purchased for approximately two thousand dollars. Since few students purchase their own bassoons, school systems usually furnish each senior high school with at least one. Normally the bassoon would be assigned to one student, and that student would keep the instrument for the amount of time that he or she remains in instrumental music, perhaps three years. During the first three years of that bassoon's life its cost would be approximately $666 per student per year. Compare that cost per student per year to the per student cost of twenty keyboards or guitars. Suppose you had only three general music classes each semester, and twenty students were enrolled in each class. One hundred and twenty different students would use the instruments during the first year. Three hundred and sixty different students would use the instruments during the first three years. The cost per student per year would be $5.56, less than the price of most textbooks.

If the cost analysis does not convince the administration that instruments for general music are affordable, ask your colleagues, students, and friends if they have unused guitars stored in their closets. You'll probably find more guitars than you need, and many owners will lend or give them to the school.

It was stated earlier that the majority of senior high school students is uninterested in the courses and organized performance groups currently offered in most music curricula. A general music class taught through performance is a viable alternative course offering for students. If music really *IS* for everyone, then secondary schools must offer music courses which provide an outlet for performance without prejudicially determining the value of the music performed or the performance.

Hunter March is Associate Professor of Music Education at the University of Texas, Austin.

A High School Music Curriculum for All Students

John Paul Johnson

Trying to conceive of a general music program at the high school level which will meet the needs of the non-performer can be a difficult task. Secondary schools have enjoyed a long tradition of musical ensembles which attract those who want to perform. For a high school music teacher who has helped in fostering this performance tradition, the prospect of developing a curriculum for those who choose not to perform can be bewildering and threatening.

Admitting that there is a need to provide music education opportunities for the non-performer leads to numerous questions. What are the musical needs of these students? How can we implement new courses into the schedule? Who will teach these classes? Who will be able to enroll in this class? The list of questions, in my circumstance, became so lengthy that I felt discouraged before beginning the task.

At the onset of developing a general music program at the Lampeter-Strasburg High School (a school of 650 students), the high school principal and the music staff agreed that our school had neglected the students who were not a part of the performing ensembles. In assuming this curricular program as part of my teaching duties, the questions which had once frustrated me provided an exciting framework upon which I could plan. I proceeded to assess the interest within the student body, evaluate my abilities and interests, and work to create a variety of courses which would embrace the student need and the constraints of the daily schedule.

The following is the roster of the music classes that are part of the school curriculum. With regard to performance demands on the students, these courses are listed in order, beginning with the least demanding.

Ninth-Grade General Music is required for all students not participating in a performance ensemble. This is the only required music course within the high school curriculum. Students in ensembles may choose this course as an elective. Each section of this class meets daily for nine weeks. A cognate within a series of required and elective mini-courses in other academic subjects, one or two sections of this class are offered each nine weeks.

Students in grades ten through twelve have five elective courses from which they can choose. **Creative Listening** is actually a music appreciation course. The title was selected when the guidance staff discovered that students would not schedule "Music Appreciation" because the name of the course sounded "boring." This class meets daily for one semester.

Folk, Rock, Jazz is designed to look at the similarities among these musical styles. Designed as a semester elective course, it has been scheduled most often as the course following *Creative Listening*.

Musical Theater is a performance, historical, and technical course. Students in this course are expected to sing and act. However, the scenes produced are not performed before the public. This semester class includes students who enjoy performing as well as those who just want to learn more about this genre.

Voice Class, which is offered two days per week for the entire year, is designed to help any student who wants to learn to sing more correctly.

Music Theory, Levels 1 and 2, is designed as a college preparation course. Students taking this class are expected to have a background on an instrument or voice. Both levels of theory are considered as different courses. However, both levels meet simultaneously three days per week for the entire year.

It is important to realize that only a portion of the course offerings can be scheduled each year. A typical year would include six to eight sections of ninth-grade general music and two or three electives.

The series of lesson plans which follows has been used in the Ninth-Grade General Music class. This class is not performance-oriented, and the ninth grade students in General Music have the least amount of interest in performing when compared with the elective course students. Therefore, these plans contrast strongly with those written for classes with performance expectations. They are, however, representative of the planning that has been done for each elective course. Activities were conceived so that all of the students would broaden their conceptual knowledge of music by listening, creating, singing or improvising on vocal sounds or percussion instruments.

LESSON 1

FOCUS: Motive
OBJECTIVE: To develop awareness of the importance of a motive within a melody.
MATERIALS: Piano, list of notated motives from familiar melodies
PROCESS: 1. Students try identifying a song by hearing the first note. Continue replaying the clue by adding one note each time until students can name the song. Repeat with other songs.

2. Introduce the concept of motive. Review the examples just heard, deciding what the minimum amount of notes would make the complete "musical idea."

3. GAME—**Name That Tune**. (Similar to well-known show.) Divide class into halves. Give one member from each team a clue as to the style or nature of the song. Students bid against each other to name the song or to have their opponents name it. The first bid begins with no more than seven notes. Each successive bid is at least one note less. When a player feels ready, he/she challenges a competitor to name the melody. If that player answers correctly, his/her team gets the point. If not, the other team receives it.

LESSON 2

FOCUS: Motive, Theme
OBJECTIVE: To develop awareness of repetition and sequence of a motive within a melody; to develop awareness of repetition of a theme within a composition.
MATERIALS: Recording, *In the Hall of the Mountain King,* by Edvard Grieg; Rhythmic pattern notated on chalkboard:

Recall *Name That Tune.* Ask what is a motive. Ask class to sing motives of familiar songs.

Ask class to study the rhythm on the chalkboard and then clap it. Class identifies the song. (*Answer: the rhythm to* Mary Had a Little Lamb.)

Determine what is the motive. (*first measure) Do the students see repetition of all or part of the first measure in the rest of the melody? (Measure 2 uses fragments of measure 1; measure 3 is nearly identical to measure 1, measure 4 uses four eighth notes like measure 1.)*

Listen to a melody which uses the same rhythm as *Mary Had a Little Lamb* and follow the rhythm on the chalkboard. Ask the class to determine if the repetitions that they found before were the same as when they heard only the rhythm. Play melody of *In the Hall of the Mountain King* on the piano. (*Measure 2 similar, measure 3 nearly exact, measure 4 different.)*

90

Invite the students to listen to the recording. They should be told that the melody that they have just heard on the piano is in the composition. Assign two tasks as they listen: Can the melody or theme be similar to a motive? How many times is the melody heard within the composition? *(Yes, a theme can be similar in use. It serves as the musical idea throughout the composition. The melody repeats eighteen times, although there are some variations in pitch and rhythm.)*

Ask the class to discuss other ways in which the composition is varied so that it does not sound like just a series of eighteen repetitions. *(Pitches change, tempo becomes faster, instrumentation changes.)*

LEARNING CENTER SUGGESTIONS

CENTER 1—EXPLORE DYNAMICS AND TEMPO.

FOCUS: Expressive quality of a composition is varied through the use of dynamics and tempo.

MATERIALS: Two tape recorders with patch cord, cassette of *In the Hall of the Mountain King*, blank cassette, worksheet.

PROCESS: 1. Students are asked to create their own composition by choosing six of the eighteen times the theme is repeated. In random order, they record these theme sections onto the blank cassette.

2. Students listen to their new recording. On a grid containing eighteen boxes (six across, three down), they mark the number of the theme in the upper row of boxes. In the next row, they mark what they consider the dynamic level to be for each theme. In the lower boxes, they mark what they consider the tempo to be.

CENTER 2—DETERMINE THE CHANGES IN THE THEME.

FOCUS: Themes varied by changes in pitch and rhythm.

MATERIALS: Cassette of *In the Hall of the Mountain King* with pauses between themes. Worksheet with numbers 1 through 18 along left side, two columns marked pitch and rhythm.

PROCESS: 1. Ask the students to listen to each statement of the theme. Using the worksheet, they indicate whether the theme has stayed the same or has changed pitch and/or rhythm.

2. If students are capable, they notate the rhythmic changes.

3. Encourage students to repeat listening to check for accuracy.

CENTER 3—DETERMINE TIMBRE CHANGES IN THE COMPOSITION.

FOCUS: Identifying instruments playing theme.

MATERIALS: Cassette of *In the Hall of the Mountain King* (as in Center #2). Gridsheet with numbers 1 through 18 on top and instruments used in composition on side.

PROCESS: 1. Students listen to each of the statements of the theme. As they listen, they mark the instruments that are playing only the theme on the gridsheet.

John Paul Johnson is completing a doctorate in Music Education at the University of Wisconsin, where he has taught secondary general music methods. Previously he taught choral and general music at Lampeter-Strasburg High School in Pennsylvania.

SECTION NINE

MULTICULTURAL MUSIC EDUCATION

Multicultural Music Education in General Music: A Perspective

Linda B. Miller

"*There is probably no other human cultural activity which is so all-pervasive and which reaches into, shapes, and often controls so much of human behavior.*"

Alan P. Merriam's statement, quoted above, emphasizes the important role of music in each culture. Music is one unique tool by which understanding and appreciation of other cultures is enhanced. Educational experiences in school music must tap and cultivate the apparent universality of music.

Study of multicultural music means incorporating both Western and non-Western musics into the classroom experience. Constituent elements (rhythm, harmony, melody, form) and expressive elements (tempo, dynamics, timbre) are inherent in the musics of many cultures. Music teachers and music programs stand to benefit from the use of non-traditional, non-Western art. If the broad purpose of the arts at the elementary and secondary school level is to prepare a cultural milieu which is richer and better, then educational experiences and exposure need to be varied.

We live in pluralistic society which continues to proliferate and mix. It seems as if American society is beyond a multicultural *awareness*. Surely students are aware of differences among the Anglo-American, Asian, Afro-American, or German students who sit in class each day. But how can music educators cultivate an understanding and appreciation of the unique cultural differences that these students bring into the classroom?

The February 1986 issue of *Music Educators Journal* focused on major approaches to music education. Of the five educators discussed, four were natives of other countries (Dalcroze, Kodaly, Orff, and Suzuki). The successful impact of their educational approaches in the United States points to the similarity of musical practices over the world. Each has a specific goal for teaching, but the instructional strategies are similar. For example, both Orff and Kodaly based certain aspects of their approaches on use of pentatonic folk songs. All of the approaches lend themselves to development of improved understanding and performance.

Others have discussed the lack of training and perspective of American music educators to teach multicultural musics. Trained and educated musicians *are* equipped to transfer their vast knowledge into teaching expressive and constituent elements of music which are inherent in non-traditional Western art. Independent study of music from other cultures should pose a challenge rather than a threat to the general music teacher. One does not have to be a native of Bali to understand gamelan music or an African to use polyrhythms effectively. Education does not commence in the college classroom. Resources, including books (reference and series), videotapes, seminars, research articles and in-service conferences, are available for music educators to expand their knowledge of world musics and materials.

Several techniques are now in use to teach multicultural music. One teacher has developed a program using familiar elements of music in new and exciting contexts. Students identify dominant elements of music from other cultures. e.g., rhythm. Rhythms are performed on classroom percussion instruments, taped, and then evaluated. Players notate their own rhythmic performance and then create improvised rhythms. The study of cultural backgrounds is correlated with social studies. A unique aspect of the program is the inclusion of field trips to galleries, museums, concert halls, and assemblies which exhibit the music and culture of peoples from over the world.

Another strategy used with upper elementary students in general music begins with discussion and exploration of students' cultural backgrounds. Students are assigned to write essays about their familial origins. They may use oral history (from relatives) and secondary sources such as encyclopedias. Examination of the music of a culture is required, i.e., the kind of music, some prominent composers, how music is used and for what purpose. Examples of the culture's music and materials are brought to class wherein comparisons and contrast to American music are made. Essays are read aloud in class, followed by questions and answers. This strategy has proven effective because students are, in reality, exploring their own cultural backgrounds. Peers have been interested in learning about each other. Parents have been eager to make contributions in terms of bringing ethnic instruments to show or play and in providing information to children. An appreciation and understanding of the music of many cultures has resulted from this strategy.

The two sample lessons which accompany this discussion illustrate other ways in which musical understanding can be developed through multicultural musical experiences.

It is important for all teachers to interpret mankind's cultural achievements—the arts. Music educators would be remiss if they left creative expression solely to teachers of art, drama, dance, or literature. There is a wealth of sources and cultures to explore and employ in the general music classroom. The challenge is ours as music educators!

Two Multicultural Music Lessons
(Black American)

LESSON 1

CONCEPT: Rhythm Syllables

CONCEPT STATEMENTS:

1) African speech rhythms have characteristic style qualities which are called "prosaic features."
2) The prosaic features may include stressed syllables, interjections, and whispering.
3) Many black American musicians—from gospel to jazz to rock—make use of prosaic features in their singing styles.

LEVEL: Secondary/General (Grades 7-12)

MATERIALS: Piano; sheet music and recording, "Greatest Love of All," Whitney Houston, Golden Torch Music Corp. (ASCAP) and Gold Horizon Music Corp. (BMI). (Some students may own this popular hit.)

OBJECTIVES: Students will:

1) Become familiar with the use of long and short syllables characteristic of African derived speech.
2) Demonstrate an understanding of prosaic features of African speech rhythms by singing "Greatest Love of All" in a similar style.

PROCEDURES:

1) Prior to the lesson have students create short poems (one verse) on topics of their choice.
2) Select several students to read their poems and point out the long and short rhythm syllables, noticing which syllables were stressed.
3) Discuss prosaic features characteristic of African music (see concept statements and references.)
4) Listen to "Greatest Love of All." Call attention to some one-syllable words that are stressed and sung as two or more syllables (extended in length by interjections, etc.); *e.g., up, place, be, long, love, to all, learn,* and *me.*
5) Determine how long and short rhythm syllables are performed in the song.
6) Teach words and melody using the piano or recording.
7) Experiment by singing the song with and without prosaic features. When singing as a group all should know how the song will be performed.

REFERENCES:

Jones, A. M. *Studies in African Music.* London: Oxford University Press, 1969.
Nketia, J. H. *The Music of Africa.* New York: W. W. Norton, 1974, 177-184.
Kauffman, R. "African Rhythm: A Reassessment." *Ethno-musicology.* 24, September 1980.

96

LESSON II

CONCEPT: Syncopation

CONCEPT STATEMENTS:

1) Most black gospel and spiritual rhythms sound similar because of syncopation.
2) In syncopation important tones are sung or played on weak beats or weak parts of the beat.
3) One can still feel or hear the underlying pulse in music which is syncopated.

LEVEL: Upper Elementary

MATERIALS: Piano; *Silver Burdett Music*, 1981 or 1985, Grade 5, books and recording.

OBJECTIVES: Students will:

1) Review 4/4 meter by clapping four quarter notes in each measure while listening to "Oh, Won't You Sit Down?" Silver Burdett Music, Book 5, p. 198.
2) Analyze the song to determine notes that fall on the beat and notes which do not fall on the beat.
3) Sing the song while clapping the steady 4/4 meter.
4) Perform the rhythm by singing and clapping.
5) Define syncopation and notate one-measure examples on the board.

PROCEDURES:

1) Briefly discuss spiritual music using the above concept statements.
2) Play the recording (or piano reduction) of "Oh, Won't You Sit Down?" and have children (a) listen for the underlying pulse and (b) clap the underlying pulse (quarter notes).
3) Analyze each measure as a group: allow children to pencil in where the four beats fall in each measure.
4) Discuss those notes which are on and off the beat, reviewing note values as you proceed.
5) Write four quarter notes on the board and contrast them with the rhythm of the first measure.
6) Teach the song using the rote-note method.
7) Sing the song as a class while clapping four steady beats per measure.
8) Ask several students to notate a syncopated measure on the board in 4/4, 3/4, or 2/4 meters.
9) Ask other children to define syncopation in their own words.
10) Sing the entire song to conclude the lesson.

Linda B. Miller is Assistant Professor of Music Education at the University of Wyoming.

Teaching Our Southeast Asian Musical Heritage

William M. Anderson

BACKGROUND INFORMATION FOR THE TEACHER AND STUDENTS

Among the world's most brilliant musical traditions is that of the Southeast Asian gamelan. Gamelan is an Indonesian word for musical ensemble. In their native setting gamelans are found in a great variety of sizes. The large gamelans are fashioned in metal, the best in bronze, and contain a number of xylophone-like instruments, gongs with raised center bosses, and drums. The ensembles may also contain several types of stringed instruments, a flute, and cymbals. Male and female vocalists may be included along with the instruments.

For many centuries gamelan music has been an integral part of Indonesian life, accompanying puppet plays and dance dramas, and being featured at temple festivals, weddings, birthdays, visits of guests and heads of state, and numerous other occasions. Hundreds of gamelans are present throughout the islands today and these orchestras are an important artistic and recreational activity for many people. Gamelan clubs are prolific and performances by the most distinguished ensembles are often heard on radio. Conservatories of music have also been established where students go to study this brilliant orchestral music. Gamelans are found not only in Southeast Asia but also throughout the United States where there are now over one hundred ensembles.

CLASSROOM ACTIVITIES

1. Have the students find the Southeast Asian country of Indonesia on a map or globe. Indonesia is comprised of more than 14,000 islands stretching nearly 3000 miles from west to east. Find Java, the most heavily populated island in Indonesia. Also find the island of Bali, the small island off the east coast of Java.

2. Make a bulletin board which includes a map of Indonesia, as well as pictures of Indonesian peoples and their country, including examples of architecture, sculpture, painting, puppetry, and music. (*National Geographic* magazines are excellent resources for good introductory articles and pictures).

3. Search out Southeast Asian people living in your community and invite them to speak to your class.

4. If you live near a college, university, or other institution having a gamelan, make arrangements for a field trip to see and hear the instruments (A list of gamelans in the United States can be acquired from the American Gamelan Institute for Music and Education, Box 9911, Oakland, California 94613.)

MATERIALS NEEDED

1. Several Orff metallophones and xylophones of different sizes.

2. Several "home-made" gongs of different sizes; fashion from different sizes of pots and pans; fashion some soft-ended mallets to strike the gongs; try for a pleasant, ringing sound.

3. One small barrel-shaped drum.

OBJECTIVES

1. Students will play the Javanese gamelan composition entitled *Bendri* (*Wedding Processional)*. They will identify the use of ostinato, the duple meter, the use of loud and soft dynamic levels, and the predominant timbre of percussion instruments.

2. Students will listen to a Balinese gamelan composition following a "listening chart" and will identify the following characteristics: strong beat, fast tempo, ornamented melody, predominant timbre of percussion instruments, duple meter.

3. Students will "sing" the gamelan composition *Bendri* (Objective 1) including the fixed melody, gongs sounding at various points in melody, and elaborating parts.

4. Students will listen to the Ramayana Monkey Chant (Ketjak) and identify some of the salient characteristics of the music.

5. Students will listen to the rock composition *Monkey Chant* by Jade Warrior and identify the Indonesian sounds.

STRATEGIES FOR TEACHING

1. Play the Javanese gamelan composition *Bendri*. (Pictures of a gamelan and of individual instruments can be found in William M. Anderson's *Teaching Asian Musics in Elementary and Secondary Schools*, available from World Music Press, P.O. Box 2565, Danbury, Connecticut 06813).

   A. Using several sizes of Orff metallophones, have several students play the following melody. As these students play the melody, have other members of the class sing the melody on a neutral syllable ("Loo"). Repeat the melody over and over until every one has learned it. Take turns with other class members playing the melody.

B. Have the students fashion three sizes of gongs, very large to small, from pots and pans to make gongs which produce a pleasant sound when struck in the middle with a soft-headed mallet. (The mallets may be made from sticks with heavy cloth covering on one end.) In a gamelan composition, gongs are sounded at various points in the "fixed" melody given above.

1) A large vertical gong, called ageng (pronounced agung; abbreviated "G"), is struck on the last note of the fixed melody of *Bendri*. Have the students play and sing the fixed melody with the large gong ageng sounding on the last beat.

2) Somewhat smaller horizontally struck gongs, called kenong (abbreviated "N"), sound on beats 2, 4, 6, and 8. Have the class fashion kenongs and play them on beats 2, 4, 6, and 8 of the fixed melody. The sounds of the kenongs should blend with the pitches on which they sound.

3) Medium sized vertically struck gongs, called kempul (abbreviated "P"), sound on beats 3, 5, and 7. Have the class fashion kempul and play them on beats 3, 5, and 7 of the fixed melody. Again, the sounds of the kempul should blend with the pitches on which they sound.

C. Practice *Bendri* with some members of the class playing and singing the fixed melody while other members of the class add the gong parts. Repeat the fixed melody and gongs over and over in ostinato fashion.

D. Add simple embellishing parts to the fixed melody and gongs. Choose several small metallophones and have students "double" the fixed melody in the following fashion:

100

E. Once the students feel comfortable just doubling the melody, ask several of them to also double and anticipate the fixed melody in the following fashion:

F. Have the class practice *Bendri* by playing the fixed melody, with gongs and embellishing parts, eight times: two times in a loud and fast style, two times in a soft and slow style, and two times in a loud and fast style, and ending two times in soft and slow style. Guide the changes from fast/loud to slow/soft by tapping the beat on a small drum.

G. If you wish to extend the piece, simply keep repeating the loud/fast and slow/soft sections with the drum indicating the changes in tempo.

2. Find the island of Bali on a map or globe. Listen to an example of Balinese gamelan music, *Hudhan Mas (Golden Rain)* (Lyrichord Records, LLST 7179, side 2, band 4). Pictures of Balinese gamelans and instruments can be found in Colin McPhee's *Music in Bali* (New Haven: Yale University Press, 1966). Place the following items on either the chalkboard or a handout for the students, and have them circle the appropriate musical events as they listen to the composition:

A. Tempo slow   or   Tempo fast
B. Strong feeling for the beat   or   Weak feeling for the beat
C. Melody unornamented   or   Melody heavily ornamented
D. Orchestra composed mostly of percussion instruments   or   Orchestra composed mostly of stringed instrument
E. Duple meter   or   Triple meter
F. Music generally reserved/restrained   or   Music generally active/spirited

3. Fashion a "vocal" gamelan in your classroom.
   A. Return to the gamelan composition *Bendri*, but this time sing the parts rather than playing them:
      1) Sing the fixed melody using the syllable "loo." Have the class repeat the melody over and over in ostenato fashion.
      2) Add the gong parts but now vocally:
         a) Gong with the sound of a low "gung" being produced by the boys on beat 8.
         b) Kenongs with the sound "nong" being produced by girls on beats 2, 4, 6, and 8.
         c) Kempul with the sound "pool" being produced by the boys on beats 3, 5, and 7.
      3) Add the simple embellishing technique of doubling the fixed melody. Choose several members of the class and have them double the melody using the syllable "lah." Then have several members of the class double and anticipate the notes of the fixed melody, again using the syllable "lah."

4. Listen to a Balinese composition entitled *Ketjak: Ramayana Monkey Chant* (from the album *Golden Rain*, Nonesuch Records, H-72028, side 2). Start 7 minutes, 20

seconds into the example.

A. This music accompanies the acting out of sections of the Hindu epic tale, The Ramayana. You may wish to read a short synopsis of the tale, by Milo Cleveland Beach, in *The Adventures of Rama* (Washington, D.C.: Freer Art Gallery, Smithsonian Institution, 1983). The setting for this music is a temple courtyard in which as many as several hundred men sit in circular fashion around a central space. In this central area, actors/dancers tell the story of the Ramayana epic in which Prince Rama's beautiful wife Sita is abducted by the evil King Ravana. The monkeys, under their leader Hanuman, assist Prince Rama in his battle with King Ravana to obtain the release of Sita. The several hundred men in the circle around the dance/drama created a large "vocal gamelan." Listen for the fixed melody which is being repeated in ostinato fashion. Then notice the sounds of vocal gongs. Finally listen to the fast elaborating parts which are being performed by many men. Place the following items on either the chalkboard or handout sheets of paper for the students asking them to circle the appropriate items as they listen to the composition:

1) Tempo slow	or	Tempo fast
2) Strong beat	or	Weak beat
3) Much repetition	or	Little repetition
4) Triple meter	or	Duple meter
5) "Vocal gamelan"	or	"Instrumental gamelan"

5. Listen to *Monkey Chant* from the rock album by Jade Warrior entitled *The Floating World* (Island Records, Inc., 7720 Sunset Boulevard, Los Angeles, California, ILSP 9290). What kinds of sounds do you hear?

Selected Readings, Recordings, and Films
BOOKS

Anderson, William M. *Teaching Asian Musics in Elementary and Secondary Schools*. Danbury, Connecticut: World Music Press, 1975. An introduction to teaching the musics of India and Indonesia.

Becker, Judith. *Traditional Music in Modern Java*. Honolulu: The University Press of Hawaii, 1980. An outstanding book on music in present-day Java.

May, Elizabeth, editor. *Musics of Many Cultures*. Berkeley: University of California Press, 1980. An excellent compilation of individual articles on nearly twenty musical traditions of the world, including Indonesia. Well illustrated. Each article contains a glossary, selected bibliography, discography, and filmography. Also includes a record of selected examples.

McPhee, Colin. *Music in Bali*. New Haven, Connecticut: Yale University Press, 1966. An outstanding survey of Balinese music. Many good black-and-white pictures.

Sadie, Stanley, editor. *The New Grove Dictionary of Music and Musicians*. London: MacMillan Publishers, Limited, 1980. Outstanding section on the music of Indonesia (Vol. 9, pp. 167-220).

Sprague, Sean. *Bali: Island of Light*. Palo Alto, California: Kodansha International Ltd., 1970. A beautiful pictorial introduction to Bali. Many outstanding color pictures are included in this paperback, including several of Balinese dances.

JOURNAL

Balungan is a publication of the American Gamelan Institute for Music and Education, a non-profit organization that sponsors courses, workshops, and concerts in the United States. *Balungen* is published three times a year and contains a variety of articles and sources of materials on gamelan. Write to the American Gamelan Institute for Music and Education, Box 9911, Oakland, California 94613.

RECORDS

Gamelan Music of Bali. Lyrichord LL7179. An outstanding recording of seven Balinese gamelan selections.

Gamelan Semar Pequlingan (Gamelan of the Love God). Nonesuch H-72046. Six gamelan selections from Bali played on the gamelan Semar Pegulingan, said by Colin McPhee to be "the most exquisitely beautiful of all the thousands of gamelans in existence on the island."

Golden Rain. Nonesuch 72028. Contains three selections of Balinese music: *Golden Rain (Hudjan Mas), Bumblebee (Tunililingan)*, and Ketjak, the *Ramayana Monkey Chant.*

Javanese Court Gamelan, Vols. I, II, and III. Nonesuch H-72044, H-72074, and H-72083. Three outstanding recordings of Central Javanese music.

Music from the Morning of the World. Nonesuch H72015. Eight selections of music from Bali. Includes a great variety of music: a lullaby sung by a young girl, a gender quartet (accompanies puppet play), monkey chant (ketjak), and several types of gamelan music.

FILMS

Miracle of Bali: Music and Dance. Xerox Educational Publications, 245 Long Hill Road, Middletown, Connecticut 06457. 45 minutes, color. An excellent introduction to several styles of Balinese gamelan music and dance.

Percussion Sounds. Churchill Films, 662 North Robertson Boulevard, Los Angeles, California 90069. 18 minutes, color. Contains a short performance of Javanese gamelan music ("Udan Mas") played by fifth-grade students.

Wayang Kulit: Shadow Puppet Theater of Java. Baylis Glascock Films, 1017 North La Cienega Boulevard, Los Angeles, California 90069. 22 minutes, color. An excellent color film showing selections of Javanese puppet theater. Includes many interesting segments of puppets and accompanying gamelan.

William M. Anderson is Professor of Music Education and Director of the Center for the Study of World Musics at Kent State University.

Southern Appalachian Mountain Music: A Means for Cultural Development

Ellen McCullough-Brabson

She was a beautiful, rich lady. One dark night, a group of gypsies came to her door and enticed her to run away with them. When her husband came home later and discovered what had happened, he was outraged. He quickly saddled his horse and searched high and low until he found his wife. When he begged her to return, she refused, choosing instead to sleep in a cold, open field and live her new life with the gypsies.

Is this a plot from a weekly television soap opera? No, it is the story line of an old Anglo-American ballad, *"The Wraggle Taggle Gypsies."* This song was preserved for many years in the Southern Appalachian Mountains. As with much of the music from this area of the United States, it still captures our imagination with its interesting tune and text.

Southern Appalachian Mountain music is a significant part of the United States' cultural heritage*. Like a patchwork quilt from the same region, Appalachian music blends a wide spectrum of color, texture, and personal expression. The study of Appalachian music gives access to a

---

*Before continuing a discussion of Appalachian music, an important point should be considered: According to *Webster's Collegiate Dictionary*, a preferred pronunciation of "Appalachia" is Appalachia (The long a, as in labor). However, the residents of this area pronounce the word Appalachia (the short a, as in add). This difference may seem insignificant, but people who live in the region value the second usage. The point is this: One should be as sensitive and inquisitive as possible when studying music from different areas or cultures. Correct pronunciation of a single word can make a difference in accuracy and authenticity.

vibrant component of America's rich musical heritage; it provides a natural springboard for the examination of other American music; it is a musically valid and interesting art form; and it offers an intriguing study of human feeling expressed through sound.

The Southern Appalachian Mountains include parts of Virginia, West Virginia, North Carolina, South Carolina, Tennessee, Alabama, Georgia and Kentucky. In the early seventeenth century, immigrants from the British Isles (England, Scotland, and Wales) began to arrive in America and settle in this area. They brought their music with them. However, because many of the immigrants were laborers, servants and farmers who were illiterate, it was not written down but was passed orally from generation to generation. Because the Southern Appalachian Mountains offered a great deal of seclusion for the pioneers, much of the music was left intact for many years. In fact, many of the people now living in the Southern Appalachians are direct descendants of the first English settlers and continue to pass on their musical heritage in the same manner as their ancestors.

Cecil Sharp, an English scholar and musician, discovered this reservoir of Anglo-American music when he first visited the Southern Appalachian Mountains in 1916 in search of British folk songs. He found many songs from the British Isles that still were being sung by the mountain people. The songs seemed untouched by twentieth-century civilization. Sharp, with the assistance of Dame Olive Campbell, collected 1,612 songs in a 48-week period. In 1932 he published a two-volume set, *English Folksongs from the Southern Appalachians,* that contained 968 of these tunes. Because these songs had not been written down before, there were many variants in tunes and texts.

Appalachian ballads, songs, games, instruments, dances and stories can richly contribute to the elementary general music curriculum. By actively experiencing Appalachian music through singing, moving, listening, creating, and playing instruments, young students will develop an understanding of and an appreciation for Appalachian music and will increase their awareness of American music.

When teaching Appalachian music to young students, the following suggestions should be considered:

1. Select authentic materials that preserve the integrity of the music.
2. Examine a broad spectrum of available resources that includes published collections, elementary music series, sound archives and individual recordings of folk musicians.
3. Teach Appalachian songs and instrumental music by "oral tradition."
4. Play for students a wide variety of recordings representing various genres of Appalachian music.
5. Teach Appalachian clog dancing, a shuffle-step type of movement.
6. Make a limberjack, an Appalachian folk instrument that imitates the movement and sound of Appalachian clog dancing.
7. Teach students to play the mountain dulcimer.
8. Examine ways in which the common elements of music (pitch, rhythm, texture, timbre, form and dynamics) are used in Appalachian music.
9. Compare and contrast Appalachian music with the music of other cultures.
10. Use visual aids such as puppets, pictures, maps and homemade storybooks to enhance the music.

These ideas have been tried and tested with children in the public schools. Recommended materials and sources are found in the selected bibliography and discography at the end of the article. Specific examples follow.

One type of song preserved in the Southern Appalachian Mountains was the ballad. Ballads were traditionally sung by an unaccompanied solo voice. They deal with a variety of topics: tragedy, humor, happiness, romance, religion, heroes, and identifiable historical events. Many of the ballads are excellent for use in the elementary music curriculum. "The Wraggle Taggle Gypsies," shown on the next page, already has been mentioned. It could be used in the classroom in both an historical and a musical context. The plot is an excellent attention-grabber and the music is interesting. The following musical characteristics are easily identified: the minor mode is used, eighth and quarter notes dominate and there are four phrases in the melody.

An effective way to introduce this ballad to children is to use finger puppets to dramatize the story. Six characters are needed: three gypsies (two women and one man,) a beautiful lady, the lord of the manor, and the servant. These visual aids assist in motivating the students to learn all of the lyrics.

Another example of an appealing ballad for young children is "Mister Frog Went A-Courting." This song has been in continuous use for over 400 years. It was passed from one generation to the next by oral tradition rather than by music notation. This accounts for the 200-plus variations of tunes and texts. Several recordings of this song illustrate the Appalachian singing style.

As a related arts project, children can illustrate each verse. These drawings can be compiled in a book that can be viewed while singing the song. A simple dulcimer accompaniment also may be added by tuning the strings to the Ionian mode and having a child strum the open strings.

Appalachian songs are also a good teaching tool. An example is the "Riddle Song." Children delight in its riddles and their resolutions. The following warm-up motivated students to learn the song. Ask children familiar riddles such as, "What bus crossed the ocean?" (Answer: Columbus.) Or, "What do you call a woman who is dating three men, all of whom are named William?" (Answer: a Bill collector.) Then present the riddles from the song: "How can there be a cherry without a stone?" "How can there be a chicken without a bone?" etc. The answers are provided in the singing of the song. Although these riddles are hundreds of years old, their appeal is as strong as ever.

There is a wonderful recording of Edna Ritchie singing the "Riddle Song." It illustrates the Appalachian style of singing and has a simple dulcimer accompaniment. Once the song has been heard, pictures of Appalachia can be shown, one for each phrase.

Many other examples of Appalachian music could be given: play-party games ("Oats, Peas, Beans"), clogging ("Sourwood Mountain"), skiffle bands ("Old Joe Clarke"), instrumental music (dulcimer and fiddles), and stories ("Sody Sallyraytus"). All of these experiences are equally important in the total presentation of Appalachian music.

The music of the Southern Appalachian Mountains is an essential ingredient of America's musical heritage and is, therefore, a meaningful part of the total multicultural music education curriculum. Cecil Sharp, in his book, *English Folk Songs from the Southern Appalachian Mountains,* supported this idea when he said "...remembering that the primary purpose of education is to place the children of the present generation in possession of the cultural achievements of the past so that they may enter as quickly as possible into their racial inheritance, what better form of music or of literature can we give them than the folksongs and folk ballads of the race to which they belong, or of the nation whose language they speak?"

The Wraggle Taggle Gypsies

English Folk Song

2. Then she pulled off her silk-finished gown,
   And put on hose of leather, O!
   The ragged, ragged rags about our door,
   And she's gone with the wraggle-taggle Gypsies, O!

3. It was late last night when my Lord came home,
   Inquiring for his a-lady, O!
   The servants said on ev'ry hand:
   She's gone with the wraggle-taggle Gypsies, O!

4. O saddle to me my milk-white steed,
   And go fetch me my pony, O!
   That I may ride and seek my bride,
   Who is gone with the wraggle-taggle Gypsies, O!

5. O he rode high, and he rode low,
   He rode through wood and copses too,
   Until he came to a wide open field,
   And there he espied his a-lady, O!

6. What makes you leave your house and land?
   What makes you leave your money, O!
   What makes you leave your new-wedded Lord?
   I'm off with the wraggle-taggle Gypsies, O!

7. What care I for my house and land?
   What care I for my money, O!
   What care I for my new-wedded Lord?
   I'm off with the graggle-taggle Gypsies, O!

8. Last night you slep on a goose-feather bed,
   With the sheet turned down so bravely, O!
   Tonight you'll sleep in a cold, open field
   Along with the wraggle-taggle Gypsies, O!

9. What care I for a goose-feather bed,
   With the sheet turned down so bravely, O!
   For tonight I shall sleep in a cold, open field,
   Along with the wraggle-taggle Gypsies, O!

107

SELECTED DISCOGRAPHY

Anglo-American Ballads. Folkways 2037.

Anthology of American Folk Music. Folkways 2951.

The Appalachian Dulcimer by Jean Ritchie: An Instruction Record. Folkways 8352.

Brave Boys: New England Traditions in Folk Music. New World Records 239.

Edna Ritchie, Viper, Kentucky. Folk-Legacy Records FSA-3.

Folk Music of the United States: Anglo-American Ballads. Washington, D.C. The Library of Congress Music Division A.AF5-L1.

Old Mother Hippletoe: Rural and Urban Children's Songs. New World Records 291.

The Ritchie Family of Kentucky. Folkways 2316.

SELECTED BIBLIOGRAPHY

Armstrong, Randall. "The Adaptable Appalachian Dulcimer." *Music Educators Journal* 66 (February 1980): 39-41.

Arnow, Hariette. *The Dollmaker.* New York: The MacMillan Company, 1954.

Brown, Tom. "Sugar in the Goard: Preserving Appalachian Traditions." *Music Educators Journal* 70 (November 1983): 52-55.

Chase, Richard. *American Folk Tales and Songs.* New York: Dover Publications, 1971.

Chase, Richard. *Grandfather Tales.* Boston: Houghton Mifflin Company, 1976.

Chase, Richard. *The Jacktales* (Folk Tales from the Southern Appalachians). Boston: Houghton Mifflin Company, 1971.

Child, Francis James. *English and Scottish Popular Ballads.* New York: Dover Publications, 1965.

Duke, Jerry. *Clog Dance in the Appalachians.* California: Duke Publishing Co., 1984.

Lomax, John A. and Alan Lomax. *American Ballads and Folk Songs.* New York: The MacMillan Company, 1934.

Ritchie, Jean. *The Dulcimer Book.* New York: Oak Publications, 1974.

Roberts, Bruce and Nancy Roberts. *Where Time Stood Still: A Portrait of Appalachia.* New York: Crowell-Collier Press, 1970.

Sharp, Cecil J. *English Folk Songs from the Southern Appalachians.* London: Oxford University Press, 1952.

Stuart, Jesse. *A Jesse Stuart Reader.* New York: McGraw-Hill Book Company, 1963.

Wigginton, Eliot, ed. *The Foxfire Book,* New York: Anchor Books/Doubleday, 1972.

Ellen McCullough-Brabson is Assistant Professor of Music Education at the University of New Mexico.

Music of Two "Southeastern" Cultures

Patricia K. Shehan

America, how you have changed! You are no longer a melting pot, but rather a mosaic of varied ethnic communities. Since mid-century, Hispanic and Asian peoples have joined those of European and African ancestry to make this country truly a global community. The American archetype as we once may have known it is gone forever, a fleeting image of our childhood years. Because of the staggering variety of ethnic groups, the "typical American" is simply not to be found.

The traditional music and artistic practices of the various national peoples living in the United States have brought the world to our doorsteps. In any large city, a sampling of customs, cuisine, and crafts can be had in shopping malls, in the nationality churches, at weekend ethnic fairs, and at various community centers. Listen to the amazing array of sounds: Mexican mariachi bands; German, Czech, and Polish polka bands; Black American gospel choirs; Carribean salsa music; chamber music of the Chinese and Japanese. The diversity of American life is clearly reflected in the music that plays on the air and in the public ear.

The musics of two of the world's regions have been bypassed for far too long. Interestingly enough, they have one common, if not musically inconsequential, element: they hail from the southeastern corners of two continents. Balkan music is found in Southeastern Europe, and the music of the Lao refugees developed in Southeast Asia. Because of the low profile which both of these musical styles have kept in school music classes, the following units of study are offered as a means of introducing elementary and middle school students to the beauty and intrigue of Music from Two Southeastern Cultures.

SOUTHEASTERN EUROPE: MUSIC OF THE BALKANS

An understanding of an exotic musical style is best begun by setting the cultural scene. A map of Europe is the starting point, searching out the "other Europe" in the lower right hand corner. The Balkans include the countries of Greece, Yugoslavia (Croatia, Slovenia, Serbia, Macedonia, Montenegro, and Bosnia-Herzogovina), Bulgaria, and Romania. Note their neighbors: Italy to the west, Hungary and U.S.S.R. to the north, and Turkey to the east. The Balkans have felt the influences of both European and Asian civilizations, a true example of cultural cross-fertilization.

Balkan music can be classified according to function: worksongs, music of the religious rituals (Christmas, Easter, St. Lazarus' Day, St. George Day), wedding song cycles, epic songs for men only, and dance music. The vocal and instrumental timbres are often strikingly Middle Eastern, with a tense and somewhat nasalized quality, and several Balkan instruments show Islamic influence, including the zornah and its double-reed relatives, the lutes of the Serbo-Croatian tamburitza ensembles, and the Bulgarian bagpipes called gaida. Melodies are often melismatic in an intriguing weave of many pitches to a single syllable. The absence of harmony is notable even on an initial hearing; instead, a heterophonic texture is common, in which performers sound simultaneous variations of the main melody. The meter of Balkan folk music is often irregular, and the five- and seven-beat rhythmic groupings are distinctively Balkan in flavor.

The following experiences, taken sequentially, are designed to develop an understanding of the music and culture of southeastern Europe.

1. Show pictures or slides of the Balkan people, depicting their colorful folk costumes, the simple stucco and earthen homes of the countryside, the horse-and-cart vehicles, the intricately woven carpets of the region, and the vestiges of Byzantine art and architecture still found in the surviving churches. Contrast this old world with the contemporary view of the urban areas, their high-rise apartments, open parks and plazas, and people in modern dress. "The Bulgarians," *National Geographic*, July 1980, is one such source of Balkan sights.
2. Listen to examples of Balkan music:
"Gaida Avasi," *Village Music of Yugoslavia*, Nonesuch H-72042. Note the timbres of the zornah (oboe) and tapan (drum), and the drone and melismatic melody of the double-reeds. The texture can be graphically illustrated on the board:

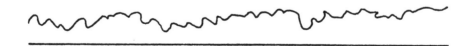

"Drachevsko," *Macedonian Songs and Dances*, Monitor MFS736. Three instruments are featured in solo or heterophonic performance: gaida (bagpipes), kaval (flute), and tambur (plucked lute). Following the gaida introduction, the ostenato rhythm ♩ ♩ ♫ ♩ can be tapped or lightly clapped while listening.

110

3. Learn this Bulgarian song, "Mountain Climbing:"

Mountain Climbing

Bulgarian folk song

Climbing up the moun-tains see the pret-ty sights be- low.
Lead the way up to the moun- tains, sing-ing as we go.

See the vil- lage hous- es scat- tered by the riv- er- side.
At the top we'll dance to- geth- er cel- e- bra- tion time.

Drum

Bell

As students listen to their teacher sing, they may pat an ostinato rhythm on their laps:

Phrase by phrase, students can learn the song by imitating their teacher.

Play the rhythmic accompaniment on two differently pitched drums. The bell ostinato can provide the tonal reference on the strong beats 1, 4, and 6.

Discuss the text. The Rhodope mountains of southern Bulgaria were traversed by Greeks, Romans, and Turks over the centuries, and are said to be vast storehouses of hidden treasures from earlier civilizations. The Rhodopes are among the most beautiful and least inhabited mountains in Europe.

4. Learn an ancient Greek folk dance:

Listen to "Kalamatiano" on *Greece is... Popular and Folk Dances*, EMI 14C 062-70007. Two violins, a guitar, and a drum play in a fast 7/8 meter: 1-2-3 4-5 6-7.

Without and then with the music, count out the meter, clapping on the accented beats:

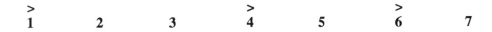

>			>		>	
1	2	3	4	5	6	7

Without and then with the music, step on the accented beats, beginning with the weight on the left foot. The movement can be chanted as follows:

Right	Left behind	Right
Left	Right behind	Left

The formation of the dance is a line, with hands held high and the elbows bent. Colorful scarves can replace held hands and provide a visual attraction in a program presentation.

SOUTHEAST ASIA: MUSIC OF THE LAO REFUGEES

South of China and east of India is the region of Southeast Asia, comprised of the mainland countries of Vietnam, Laos, Cambodia, Thailand, Burma, and Malaysia, and including the island countries of Indonesia and the Philippines. Its geographical setting explains the influences of its powerful neighbors on philosophy, architecture, legendry, dance, drama, and music. A cultural exchange of artists and scholars from India and China brought an infiltration of Hindu and Buddhist traditions for at least 1400 years. Still, unique cultural practices emerged in the southeast corner of Asia, with the orchestras of gongs and xylophones leading the way a key symbols of the region.

As a result of political upheaval in their Asian homeland, the Lao, Vietnamese, Cambodian, and Hmong Peoples have brought vestiges of their culture to North American re-settlement communities. Refugees from Laos bring the rich musical traditions of the Southeast Asia. The Lao classical court orchestra resembles those of Thailand, with its wooden xylophones, dimpled gongs, cymbals, and drums. Many layers of sounds occur simultaneously, and the initial reaction is that "these instruments are not playing together." Rather, the heterophonic effect is caused by many simultaneous views of the melody, which sounds uniquely different in each instrumental idiom. Court music was rarely heard by middle-class and common folk, and the majority of Lao traditionally danced and sang to a free-reed instrument known as a kaen. Its drone-like harmony is pleasing, and its harmonica timbre is familiar to westerners. As the national instrument of Laos, the kaen accompanies folk songs, sung stories, and courting poems. Both classical and folk music is based in pentatonic scales and set in duple meter.

The general music class can be the site of a number of experiences for nurturing a tolerance and taste for the music and culture of Southeast Asia, and in particular, the Lao refugees.

1. Show the films "Mekong" (Shell Oil, 25 minutes, color, grades 4-9) or "Boy of Southeast Asia" (University of Michigan, 17 minutes, color, elementary school) which introduce the fishing and farming communities, the family life, and the schooling of children in rural Thailand, Laos, and Cambodia before the political unrest of the last decade. "Thais Seek Charmed Lives" (*Asia*, May/June 1980) and "The Desperate Struggle to Save Cambodian Culture" (*Asia*, September/ October 1980) provide photographs and background information.